ALAN BIGGINS

SELLING FRENCH DREAMS

Kirkdale Books

Reviews of 'A Normandy Tapestry'

A Normandy Tapestry...

• Has been serialised in *Living France* Magazine

And has had the following reviews:

'Humour ....village life ... history ....everything of Normandy is here.'
France magazine

'Every page is an eye-opener ...rarely does a book get so under-the-skin of rural France. A cracker.'
Richard Binns, best-selling author on France.

'I can reveal the answer to the problem of no television when you go on holiday. Take *A Normandy Tapestry*.'
France In Print.

'A magical evocation of an area and its people.'
Derek Jameson

'Informative and immensely enjoyable. Essential reading for the visitor to Normandy. A classic of its kind.'
George East - La Puce publications

Visit www.normandy-tapestry.com to find out more.

Introduction

I left my first book, *A Normandy Tapestry* at a point where my family was settled in France. My wife, Ann, was holding the reins of the family and our children, Alice and David, were at a French school. I was working for an estate agent, having failed by a whisker to pass my exams in French. A Jack Russell puppy was yapping about my ankles. That was seven years ago.

I would like to thank the many kind readers who have written to me about the book. I am very happy that they enjoyed, were often amused by, and sometimes learned a bit from my mixture of tales of property, my family, and the people and places of beautiful rural France.

Their reactions - and their requests to know 'what happened next?' - have encouraged me to write this book. My aim in writing it has been quite simple - to state at any rate! To write a book that you will not want to lend out - but which you will want to recommend to your friends!

And there is another reason why I have written this book. For many who try it, the French dream goes wrong and they return to Britain within a couple of years. This bald fact represents a great deal of misery and waste to those concerned. As the same things go wrong time and time again, much of that suffering is avoidable. I hope, and trust, that the chapter: 'The Dangerous Crossing', and the appendix, will save some of my readers some of that suffering.

The Jack Russell is older now, and curled up snug on the bed as the winter storm blows in across the field. Apart from that, quite a lot has happened since I last put pen to paper ... ...

FOR
The reader
....and my family

Published by KIRKDALE BOOKS
Great Horwood,
Milton Keynes,
Buckinghamshire. MK17 0QQ

First printed: May 2002
ISBN: 0-9523149-5-9
Copyright: Alan Biggins 2002. All rights reserved.

Made and printed in Great Britain by:
Cromwell Press
Trowbridge
Wiltshire
Typeset in Arial 11.5

British Library Cataloguing in Publication Data:
A catalogue record is available for this book from
the British Library.

Thanks: René and Thérèse Grente.
         Monsieur Brochard and the staff at Percy school.
         Suzanne McCafferty. Roger & Cath Ward.
         George East. Charles Arnold. Colin Bell.

Illustrations: Tony Beesley (cover). Erica Stokes.

Contents

Part 1: Property

A typical country 'Notaire's house' (see chapter two) of the type I love so well. This one cost around £15,000 and had over two acres of land.

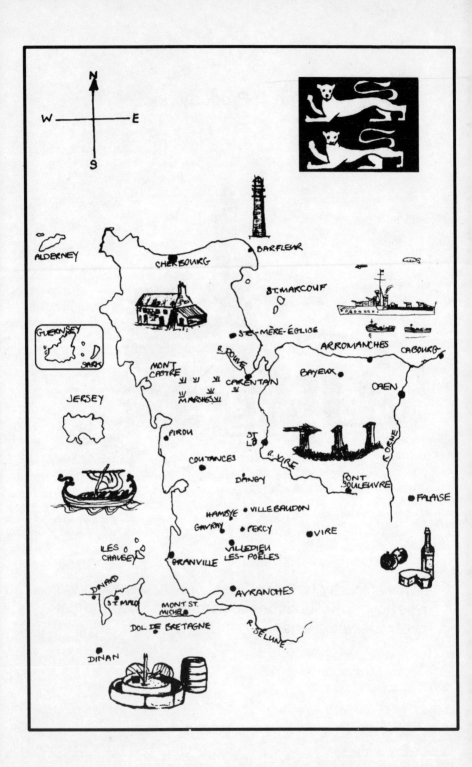

ALDERNEY

BARFLEUR

CHERBOURG

ST. MARCOUF

GUERNSEY

SARK

STE-MÈRE-ÉGLISE

ARROMANCHES

CABOURG

R. DOUVE

MONT
CASTRE

CARENTAN

BAYEUX

CAEN

JERSEY

MARSHES

PIROU

ST.
LÔ

COUTANCES

R. VIRE

PONT
SOULEUVRE

FALAISE

D'ANGY

R. ORNE

HAMBYE

VILLEBAUDON

ILES O
CHAUSEY

GAVRAY

PERCY

VIRE

VILLEDIEU
LES-POÊLES

DINARD

GRANVILLE

ST. MALO

AVRANCHES

MONT ST.
MICHEL

DOL DE BRETAGNE

R. SÉLUNE

DINAN

Morning. Contrasting characters.
The builder's bargain. Evening.

There was a slight rawness to the morning. Autumn was
advancing. A thick mist was rolling in from the *bocage* - that
system of small fields, high hedges and shady rutted tracks
that typifies Normandy. It was getting too cool to eat breakfast
outside any more.

We had been in France for about six months and our days
were beginning to take on a pattern. The children, David and
Alice, had been across the road to René and Thérèse's - our

neighbours - farm and collected a litre of milk in the aluminium milk can - the *pot au lait*. With typical kindness, Thérèse had also popped a new-laid egg and two sweets in the lid.

Our lunatic Jack Russell, Flavie (named by Alice in honour of one of her classmates), had thrown herself in frenzy against the front door at the sound of the *facteur* putting our post (a handout from the Monoprix supermarket and a black-edged envelope advising us of the death of a neighbour in the Commune) in the box.

I had poured some hydraulic fluid into the innards of my equally lunatic French car, leaving it to lurch from its knees to its feet like a colicky horse while I skirted round the well, through the backdoor, past the disjoncteur (fuse box) of evil intent, kissed Ann goodbye and left her to the morning-time coo and witter of the house.

"I can't find my book (hat/coat/skirt/head)."

"What do you expect love, the house is a tip because people leave stuff everywhere. It's in the bathroom, on the clothes basket, where you left it."

My work had taken on a pattern too. I would either go out to take-on more houses or - more often lately - to show those houses to prospective buyers. Dick, my English boss at the immobilier (estate agency) where I worked, had begun to put more customers my way. It was a bit late in the season for selling, but it had taken me a long time to find the hundred or so houses that I needed to give a cross-section of interesting properties.

This morning I was meeting a customer, a builder from Sussex called Mr Bignall. Sometimes, as today, I would meet my clients at the agency, sometimes the agency would send me a fax and I would meet them in a café. Neither arrangement was very satisfactory. I reflected, as I always did when I made the long drive, on how badly I needed my own office - the office which Dick had promised me when he took me on. That, in turn made me think about Dick and Monsieur Pierrot. I smiled, as I usually did, as I thought of the contrasting characters of my two bosses.

Dick had sold me our house. Then - mainly because I spoke French well - he had offered me a job. He hadn't needed to ask me twice. I was looking for a way of supporting myself during my French studies (of which more later). I'm a hard worker and a good one, so I had expected to 'get by' one way or another; but to be offered a job where I would be using French so much, and so colloquially, seemed like a gift from heaven.

Dick was a go-getter. He was about fifty years of age and had retired to Normandy, but he couldn't keep still. So, some eighteen months earlier, he had offered his services to Monsieur Pierrot, the owner of the agency, to sell houses to the British.

Dick was charming, a grafter, and a born salesman. It was a winning combination. Business had gone mad. He had, in his own words, 'pulled the agency back from the brink,' and was now doing by far the greater part of that agency's business - and working all the hours God sends.

Hence his need of help.

He had employed me, along with two others, to open offices in new areas. He had assigned me a 'patch' about forty miles from head office, in the general area of Mont St Michel. Expansion was in the air. It was exciting.

Dick was full of energy, full of ideas; for example, he had written to the ferry companies to try to get discounts for our customers, and he had built up a directory of tradesmen who those customers could use for renovations or repairs. He and I had searched 'my' area for suitable premises for an office, and we had short listed four properties. Dick had given the list to Monsieur Pierrot months ago. Since then, Monsieur Pierrot had done nothing about it.

If that was the major frustration I felt about Monsieur Pierrot, for Dick I fancy that it was just one of a long list. Seldom have I seen such a contrast of characters. If Dick was dynamic, the owner of the agency was very much 'old-school'. He was a man of around sixty, very thin, spare and tall. He was a little like a predatory bird. There was something strangely likeable about him; but he was not what you would call 'hands-on'. He very rarely took customers to see properties, and usually only came into the office in the evenings. He paid for the premises and a receptionist, and in return took a large slice of the earnings, which, as I've said, were mainly generated by Dick. He was, to all intents and purposes, a sleeping partner.

I don't think that Dick found this an entirely satisfactory way of working. His own style was hard work and leading by example. Above all he was a straight forward, results-driven businessman. He was a trifle blunt. It was by running his own business in England that he had managed to save enough to retire to France. Like any businessman he owed his success to many factors, among them, 'running a tight ship, without waste, passengers, or unnecessary overheads'. In Britain, of course, the obvious thing for a man of his ability to do would have been to employ a competent assistant and set up his own agency.

Estate agency isn't particularly complex. The difficult bits are the legal aspects, but these are not the immobilier's concern, they are the notaire's (solicitor), and a notaire has to be used in any property transaction. Estate agency in France is, however, a highly regulated profession. To become an estate agent, you need a *Carte Professional.* Mr Pierrot had that piece of paper (the prerequisites for which I was later to learn in a rather dramatic fashion), Dick did not.

I grumbled a bit more to myself as I parked the car. Now I had to pick up my customer and back-track on myself for forty miles to take him to my 'patch'. I would need to fill the car up on the way. All this travelling wasted so much time and money! (we agents paid for our own petrol and worked completely on a commission basis: no sale, no pay). I would have to chase-up Monsieur Pierrot again about that office!

I went into the agency. The receptionist smiled:

"*Ton client est ici, Alain, mais malheureusement tous les bureaux sont occupés.*"

All the offices were full. Typical! We 'new bugs' were at the bottom of the pecking-order for space and often had to conduct our business in the reception area. Another reason why I needed that office. But enough of office politics; to work!

I showed Mr Bignall enough of my property portfolio to convince him that I had houses that he would like to see, then we got into my car.

My customer was dressed in clean jeans and a short sleeved shirt, and carried with him a notebook and pen. He was a tall, slim, man of about thirty-five with fine steady eyes, who had a clear, uncomplicated look about him. He was the kind of man who you would trust at first sight; and although I have since come to mistrust snap summaries of character, in his case you wouldn't have been mistaken.

He was reluctant to talk at first. I could see that he was wary of me. That had been a novel experience for me when I started work as an estate agent, but I had soon got used to having to win my customers' trust. I spoke to him a bit about the area and asked him about himself.

A builder's work can be seasonal, so he was looking, as many a small builder was, for something that he could buy cheap, work on during odd weekends in the summer and more intensively during the winter. When he had done it up, he would then either let it out or sell it on. He wasn't sure which yet. The idea of a place of his own was appealing; but you could never be sure how cash-flow would go. But he had to get a property cheap. The maximum that he was prepared to pay, including all fees, was £25,000; though he didn't really want to pay more than £20,000, if he could help it.

I told him that he had come to the right place. I was virtually the only English agent in the area, and, working with notaires as I was (which I'll explain a bit later), I had access to a virtually untapped pool of affordable places, full of character, which usually needed a bit of renovation.

"Yeah, I'm sure you'll 'see me right squire,'" he said sarcastically. "I've been around a bit you know. Let me make it clear." He pronounced the words individually. "I don't want you quoting one price to me, another to the seller, and then pocketing the difference."

Mr Bignall was going to be a difficult customer to win round, but this was an odd suspicion, and one which was very easy to allay. I explained to him that the price was clearly stated in the sale's agreement - the *Compromis de vente* - which was a legal document. There would be no trickery.

We drove along in silence.

We stopped briefly at my house, which was on the way, so that we could look properly at my (best) book of property details and make a selection of places which he liked the look of. He chose four.

"Can I add one of my own?" I asked him. "If it's all the same to you, I'd like to start with this one." I showed him a photograph. He nodded dubiously. "I suppose so."

So we began with 'my choice', three adjoining houses, the end of a terrace of four, in a village between Avranches and Vire. The terrace stood back from the main road (if you could call it that, with perhaps half a dozen cars per hour). The access road to the houses went round a small patch of land which was laid to vegetables and had chickens running on it. The houses themselves were in irregular rose-granite, each of two stories, topped by a gable, in which was a further window.

To describe one is to describe all. A large room downstairs, five metres by four with great smoke-blackened beams and a huge open granite fireplace. Over and to each side of the fireplace, two wooden 'lugs' stuck out from the wall. These are commonplace in such houses - obviously they were to support something - although what that something was, I have never been able to find out. Behind this room, underneath the stairs, was a W.C.

On the first floor were two bedrooms, separated by wooden plank walls. The attic (reached by somewhat rickety stairs) made another good-sized room, although foreshortened at the front and back by the fall of the eaves. Behind each house there was a yard and a small shed. The vegetable garden in front belonged to the three houses.

Two of the houses were joined by an internal door, obviously unopened for many years. I pointed out to Mr Bignall that the slate roofs were in good condition and would not need renewing. The three houses cost around £20,000 . When the fees were added, the total was about £24,000.

The builder looked round the houses thoughtfully. He took out his notepad and began to write.

The other properties which we saw that day were much of a pattern, barns or run-down houses, places which needed an awful lot of work. All needed re-roofing. Mr Bignall asked me a lot of questions about planning consent, local suppliers of wood, cement, stone, brick, windows and the like. I had my answers ready.

A great advantage of having a personal computer and laser printer, rather exotic items in rural Normandy in the 'nineties, was that I had prepared quite a lot of material for potential buyers. The estate agency fees are extraordinarily high in comparison with British ones, and my attitude was that 'cost plus' should mean 'service plus'.

I offered Mr Bignall two leaflets, one about planning law, which he accepted, the other about renovation costs, which he waved aside.

As we drove about, my customer referred again and again to the terrace of three houses which we had first visited.

Sometimes he asked me questions: what were the facilities in the village again? (a general-purpose store, a baker and a bar). Was there any call from holiday companies for large accommodation, such as the three houses together would represent? (Yes).

Sometimes, he spoke almost to himself. "No damp, and the roof's good. That's important if I'm working in winter. I could live in one part while I did the rest of it up. When I finished one house, I could let it out and move onto the next one. I could even sell one if I wanted and still have two more...." Then he turned to me:

"Would these places sell if they were done up?" I assured him that they would; but he would need to be a little careful about the legal entity with which he bought them, and how and

10

when he sold them. It was all to do, of course, with tax. I had written a leaflet about it. By no means exhaustive, but it should help. I gave him a copy of that as well.

"You're a walking ruddy library," he grunted as he carefully folded the document and put it in his breast pocket to join the earlier one.

In showing Mr Bignall the terrace, I was following a bit of good advice that Dick had given me about selling property; "Show them the best place first." The customer would then automatically use it as a yardstick, keeping it always in his mind. By the time we had gone round the other houses, he had become more and more excited about the terrace, as I had thought he might.

My customer was right to be excited. In his place, I would have been excited too. Three houses in good condition for about £8,000 each! Even for France, that was a gift. If he bought and renovated them, he would probably be able to sell each of them for more than the price that he paid for them all. Even taking into account the cost of renovation, he still stood to make a substantial profit.

We went back to have a second look, Mr Bignall all the while muttering to himself and making notes: "half an hour to the sea .....private garden .....flexible accommodation ....in village with amenities." He only needed to toss in 'in beautiful tranquil area' and 'stone's throw from spectacular Mont St Michel' and he could have been an agent himself.

After seeing the terrace for the second time, the builder suggested stopping at a bar. He had been on his nerves that day, hardly surprising as he was considering a big investment, both in time and money. He bought two beers. We sat outside in the warm autumn sun.

"O.K." he said. "I'd like to put an offer in. I'd like to buy the whole place, fees included, for twenty thousand pounds. Will they sell for that?"

I shrugged. It was, of course, an impossible question. "That depends. I don't know the sellers personally, only their notaire. How much will you go to if they don't?"

He turned to me, suspicious again. "You don't think I'm going to tell you that do you?"

I sighed. "Be reasonable. How can I negotiate if I don't know what's on your mind. Whose side do you think I'm on?"

He scowled. "Your own I should think, if not, the sellers'."

It was a common misconception. I raised my beer glass to my companion: "The agent is on the side of the person who pays his fees. That, Mr Bignall, is you."

And then, much to my surprise, he smiled. It was the first smile I had seen from him all day. "You know, Mr Biggins, I think I trust you. With all your handouts you're more like an information office than an estate agent. You ought to make a book of all this. O.K. If I need to, I'll go to the full asking price."

Back at the office, I relayed the builder's bid to the owners' notaire. The owners themselves were not contactable at such short notice, so Mr Bignall had to go back to England and stew a while (the offer was subsequently accepted).

It came as no surprise that I was unable to track down Monsieur Pierrot, to discuss my promised office. It would just have to wait yet another day. I went home.

Our evenings, too, had taken on something of a pattern. Flavie, our puppy, daughter of Zoe, neighbour René's Jack Russell bitch, had to be walked. Originally we had hoped to simply let her wander over the garden, but in common with most of her breed, she had the terrible habit of raising merry hell if anyone had the cheek to walk, cycle or drive past. Although this was a rare enough occurrence, it was still likely to lead to nipped neighbours or a squashed dog. She also had a tendency, as puppies will, to bolt. So she stayed inside unless supervised.

And so Operation Dog Walk commences.

The troops are marshalled. We all put on our *bottes* (Wellingtons, although I suppose it would not be wise to use the word around here). David puts a bow that I have made for him out of a branch and a piece of string over his shoulder. We are off.

We turn left out of the house and head down the lane. The lanes round the house are, as most lanes are in Normandy, sunken. The rock (soil would be a better word for it, it's so soft), is sandstone and shale. When a track has been started, wet weather turns it into the bed of a stream. Erosion continues the work. A thousand years of such action explains why the banks above the roads and tracks are now higher than a man. And I suppose that these ways have been in use at least a thousand years. Maybe a good deal longer. The land rises up to Mont Robin, the second highest hill in the Department (pretty low at that, only about 270 metres), which I think had a signalling station on it in Roman times.

The first part of our walk is on the single-track road leading to the neighbouring hamlet of five houses. Even this is sunken, for although it was metalled perhaps fifty years ago, that is only a very small part of its history. The road skirts our property in a dip, René's fields rising to the right. We go over the stream where the muskrats live. Then we turn left onto The Muddy Path. This, again, is a sunken lane, but it has never been made-up for vehicles. It is over-arched by trees and bushes and is only ever used by the local farmers when they put their cows in the fields which lie alongside.

This, as I have said, is the bocage, the landscape that gave the Allies such trouble after the Normandy landings. And this particular area was very hotly contested, changing hands nine times. Impassable to tanks, impossible to spot from the air, a couple of well-sited guns (and the Germans had a genius for such things) gave all the advantages to the defender. Thankfully, things are a bit more peaceful nowadays. The only raid we have in mind tonight is on René's field.

Today, mercifully, the track is not too bad and I don't need to carry anybody, not even Flavie, over the muddy bits. The ferns are still green in this dark tunnel. They have not started to die back yet. There are brambles and nettles too, but the cows keep the track clear enough to use.

"Flavie, Flavie!" David, trailing slightly, is the only one who notices that the dog is missing. She often does this, darting off after the scent of a fox, or a badger, or a rabbit or hare. This is the signal for five or ten minutes calling until she gets tired of the game and comes back. I find this very wearisome, but am voted down and told not to be so miserable.

After half a mile or so we leave The Muddy Path and come onto another very minor rutted road. As we walk along it we come up to an ancient stone house, in front of which a man is tending his vegetables. He is dressed in the regulation 'blues' of the French countryside. We have nodded to him in passing often enough and wished him good evening, but he has never spoken. It is a surprise, then, when he leaves his beans and makes his way over.

"*Ah, Monsieur et Madame Bee-geen.*" The bush telegraph works very well here. "How are you settling in?"

We tell him that we are very happy.

"Your orchard. It has many trees."

14

"Yes." I reply proudly. "One hundred. Only a couple of eaters though. All the rest are cider apples."

"Ah yes, cider apples. I suppose that you have no use for them. I will take them away if you wish."

I bet he would! "Well, we have promised them to the co-operative. They will give us a good price for them."

The conversation peters out and we move on. It is somehow refreshing to see motives as clear as his. Even the kids are alive to it.

"He is very interested in apples." Says Alice. "Our Monsieur Pomme."

The name sticks and subsequently we will find it hard not to giggle as we pass his house.

Now we are coming into Villebaudon, a village on a crossroads of main roads, north to south, east to west. Villebaudon has two cafes, a post office (when it's open) and a shop. This is our destination. We buy a packet of sweets (Krema) for the children and a bottle of beer for me. I'm not a great wine drinker and we can get all the cider we want from René.

Now we set off home.

"I've learnt a new song at school." Says Alice. She sings it in the clear, piping voice of a seven year old:

"Au clair de la lun-ah
j'ai peté en eau
ca a fait des boul-ah
c' était rigolo."

(In the light of the moon, I tooted in the bath. It made some bubbles, which was funny).

"That's a bit naughty," says Ann, scandalised. We go past Monsieur Pomme's house in a fit of giggles. David wants to threaten him with his bow, but I stop him. Monsieur Pomme glowers, sure we are making fun of him.

Now we are back onto The Muddy Path. It is getting dark under here as dusk approaches. We must hurry, as we have a job to do before getting home. We climb up the bank and into a field. It is one of René's fields and we are here to collect blackberries. The blackberries in France are bigger and lusher than they are in England and it does not take the four of us long to fill a couple of plastic containers, although most of what Alice and David pick seems to go in their mouths, on their clothes, or to Flavie, who also likes the fruit.

Ann will be baking apple and blackberry pie and making jam, some of which she will give to Thérèse. I eye up the rose-hips. Sometimes at this time of year I make up some rose-hip syrup for the children and I to take over winter. But it's getting late.

"Flavie! Flavie!" It is noticeably darker in the hollow of The Muddy Path now and we are silent as we make our way back to the road. We cheer up as we come onto it.

"Do you want to hear my other song?" Says Alice.

We are a bit dubious about that, but it turns out to be a marching song, a bit like 'Ten green bottles', counting down from ten to one, repeated to taste:

> "Dix kilomètres à pied,
> ca roul-a, ca roul-a,
> dix kilomètres à pied,
> ca roul-a sous les pieds.
> Neuf kilomètres à pied... "

("Ten kilometres on foot, it rolls, it rolls, ten kilometres on foot, it rolls beneath the feet.")

Soon we are all singing it. We have been out for over an

hour and we haven't seen a car.

The stars are coming out as we arrive home. It is chilly. Alice and David are sent across the road to René and Thérèse's farm to leave the *pot au lait* outside the milking parlour to be filled in the morning. Their evening task. Then Ann gets them ready for bed while I go from room to room opening each window, leaning out and pulling the shutters closed. Far too dangerous a job for the children.

Now it is time for a story. The three of us snuggle into bed. This evening, I read them a French tale, about a carthorse pulling a wagon up a steep hill and a fly who buzzes constantly in the beast's ear. The sweating horse is enraged. The fly is proud of the assistance that he has given the horse. "We did it!" he says when they get to the top. There is madness in the horse's eyes.

Ann lights the fire. It is a wood-burning stove which we haven't used much before. I need to go and cut some more wood. I walk across the gravel path, past the deserted chicken run and into the open-fronted barn where I put on the light. An owl has begun to hoot. Behind me, the house is in darkness, all shuttered up.

I take down the big saw from its nail on a rafter and start to saw up one of the long pieces of wood - like pit props - a pile of which lies beyond the orchard. It is hard work. I stop and take a piece of candle wax from a shelf and rub it up and down the blade to make it run more easily. Ah, that's better! The work begins to take on a rhythm that is still in my head. I start to sing....

"Dix kilomètres à pied, ca roul-ah, ca roul-ah..."

The owl hoots in protest.

SELLING FRENCH DREAMS

MISTLETOE

Pond life. The notaire's office.
Out with the Averys.
Playing the 'everything' game.

My ideal house would have a flat roof on which I could lie on
a summer's night to watch the stars, two staircases (so that
the children could play hide and seek, as I used to do in my
grandfather's house), and a stream to lull me off to sleep with
the sound of running water (wind through trees is nearly as
good).

I have never lived in a house which had any of these
'features'; and putting them in is generally impractical or
ruinously expensive. One luxury we have always allowed
ourselves, however, is a pond.

The pond that we had made was on the edge of the front lawn. Beyond it lay the gap in the hedge through which, before we put a wire across it, René's cows used to make a break into our garden.

Of course, with children about, we'd had to plan the pond very carefully. They weren't toddlers anymore, so we didn't have to fence it off, but we had used slopes and ledges. We would have done that even if we had had no children. Small creatures, such as hedgehogs, voles and shrews, are not too keen on sheer sides either. They are better suited to the grave digger than to the pond maker.

Taking the pond off the drawing board and making it a reality had been a fairly major undertaking. It was back-breaking work digging a hole twelve feet long and six wide at the surface, which then went down, in a series of ledges, to a (maximum) depth of three feet.

Then there was vegetation. There are not many garden centres (actually none) in rural Normandy; but there are plenty of bogs and streams, so the four of us had had lots of mucky journeys with buckets and nets to find the plants needed, (and whatever insects, fish eggs and snails might be sticking to them) and lots of sessions at the kitchen table with wildlife books trying to identify what they were.

After that it just got better and better. The miniature world became more and more engrossing as it matured. Wildlife gradually colonised it: pond skaters, water beetles, frogs, toads and newts.

There is nothing quite like watching the goings-on of pond life to take you away from the stress and immediate worries of your own existence. Gazing into its depths, all the mystery and drama and sorrow and excitement of existence can be seen. Sex, birth, murder and death.

When we were able, we liked to take breakfast by the pond, as we were doing this morning. Crusty French bread, Norman butter, *Bonne Maman* jam, orange juice and fruit. The summer was dying. It was to be the last day of the year which was warm enough to allow us to eat breakfast outside.

Then it was time to take the children to school (in the village of Percy. The village was the origin of the Christian name and not the other way around, but I would have to take you back into Norman history to explain why).

Today I was to take out an English couple who had gone directly to a notaire. To understand what that means, I need to explain a little about the French property market, and more specifically the roles of the immobilier and the notaire. (For those who have read my previous book and have a feeling of *déja vu* in the next two pages, please accept my apologies. I shall not be repeating myself again.)

Looking for a house in Britain is, of course, easy. You simply breeze into a shop, look at what's on the wall and pick out a few details for closer perusal at home.

That is not the way of it in rural France.

Most French country properties are sold by notaires. The notaire is a government-appointed official who mixes the duties of a solicitor and an estate agent. He (I have never met a female notaire) is a highly respected figure in the rigidly-hierarchical social structure of the French countryside. He is commonly addressed as *maitre*.

Apart from the fact that small towns do not have immobiliers anyway, there are several advantages to buying from a notaire. Firstly, it's cheaper. Notaires' negotiation fees are set by the state. Typically, an immobilier, who can set his own fees, will charge twice as much (generally between 5 and 10 percent).

Then there is conservatism. Many country folk would no more dream of asking an agent to sell their house than they would of asking a witch-doctor to hear their confession. So the rural notaire often has a far better selection of 'character' houses than the agent. This, of course, is precisely the type of property that the British buyer is normally interested in. The French, on the other hand, are usually not. They will be much more likely to be searching out modern houses. As the notaire is unlikely to have too many British visitors, there is a reasonable chance that he will have a good selection of bargains. Occasionally those bargains are astounding, as I will illustrate later.

But there are drawbacks. The notaire's office often takes a bit of finding. It is (like much of rural France) closed between twelve and two. Then, in order to see his 'black book' of property details, it is usually necessary to see the notaire himself. This means making an appointment or waiting, which is fine if one has time to spare, but not much good if one is on holiday and in a rush.

When one finally does get to meet the notaire, he is generally a very pleasant and knowledgeable man. However, he does not speak English (there must be exceptions but I have never met one).

The notaire's property details (in French, obviously) vary from the hand-written to those produced on a laser printer. Frequently they are abbreviated: *'toit ard, verg, F4'* ('slate roof, orchard, F4'). F4? What the 'F' means I have never discovered, but the '4' refers to the number of main rooms.

As this system is a century or two old, kitchens, WC's and bathrooms do not get included in the count. A house, then, will sometimes be simply described as having four rooms. If further information is given, it never includes room dimensions.

Sometimes the information can be even scantier. For example:
"Maison en pierres couverte en ardoises -Verger
Prix: 100,000 Frs   Frais: 20,040 Frs"
(Stone house with slate roof - Orchard.
Price: 100,000 francs Fees: 20,040 francs)

The service of *Maitre le notaire* is, not surprisingly, geared to French expectations, not British ones. To those who are used to a 'self-service' approach and have neither much time nor a good command of French, a visit to his *étude* is much more likely to lead to confusion and frustration than the unearthing of treasure. This is where the British agent, if he is astute, can score heavily. Given that the notaire usually has a good stock of houses, it is not unusual for that agent to do a deal with him so as to get access to his properties.

The immobilier who I worked for had done deals with a number of notaires. The visit I was to make today, however, was a slightly unusual case. My agency's agreement with this particular notaire was only a couple of days old, so I didn't know his property. In fact getting to know his houses was going to have been my job for the day. The English customers who I was to meet there, Mr and Mrs Avery, had forestalled me slightly, having gone directly to the notaire on the previous day. The notaire, speaking no English, had asked me to meet them today, to take them to view 'his' properties.

While the notaire conducted his other business in his *étude* (selling property was a minor part of his job and one that he did not concentrate on), the Averys and I sat in the waiting room and thumbed through his books of properties. In the other seats in the waiting area sat a farmer, two elderly ladies and a young man with a large black dog.

SELLING FRENCH DREAMS

The Averys were probably in their mid-thirties. Mr Avery - Howard - had an expensive cream-coloured jumper draped over his shoulders, the sleeves tied lightly in front of his neck. He had rather sharp features, piercing eyes and the marked habit of thrusting his face slightly forward as he spoke, which added to his air of a man who was used to getting his own way. Mrs Avery - Emma - was an attractive woman with beautiful brown eyes and a lovely smile. She had an aura of calmness about her. Like her husband, she was casually but smartly dressed.

Showing the notaire's house details to the Averys posed some problems. If you're serious about selling property, then part of the art, and courtesy, of the job is in the intelligent display of your portfolio. The efficient agent in rural France will have a mass of property on his books, far more than one file can hold. So he will have a second and perhaps a third book, which the customer rarely gets to see.

In the second book will be the houses which are not to the British taste, and those that the agent knows that there is a problem with. There are always problem houses. One of mine, for example, was owned by six squabbling siblings, only four of whom were keen to sell, only three of whom were easy to get hold of, and one of whom was (permanently) on her deathbed.

'Book two' will also contain details of those houses which are not in the British price bracket (too expensive, never too cheap!), the houses that are overpriced, those where access is difficult to arrange, and the badly positioned. One house of mine was situated next to a railway siding, another beside a cement factory, a third opposite a very smelly chicken farm.

'Book one' is where the best stuff is, filed in price sequence. That's the way estate agents do it. Notaires, on the other hand, often hold their property details in arrival sequence, latest stuff at the top, oldest at the bottom. Such was the case today. Cheap and expensive, ruins and manors, farms and commercial premises, all were jumbled together willy-nilly.

My customers made their selection, which were then vetted by the notaire's clerk. *Bien sur*, there were complications. Of the half-dozen houses which interested the Averys, the notaire held the keys for only one. Three of the remaining sellers were uncontactable, and the other two could be visited, but only after lunch.

The notaire's assistant arranged the afternoon visits. She would be able to come with us to see those two houses. The first house however - the one for which we had the keys - the Averys and I were to visit by ourselves.

As often happened in these exchanges, the woman - Emma in this case - had understood much of the French conversation between the notaire's clerk and myself, while the man, Howard, had understood little. I could see that this annoyed him. He saw no reason to wait until we had left the notaire's office before giving vent to that annoyance:

"Bloody foreigners couldn't organise a piss-up in a brewery!"

The young man with the large black dog frowned at Mr Avery. The large black dog gave a sharp bark. I grinned weakly at both of them.

"Take it easy darling," said Emma softly. Then, with a disarming smile, she turned to me: "I hope that you can find the house. You've never been there before, have you?"

It was true that I had never visited the property. "I'm sure there'll be no problem there," I said, a little primly, "I know exactly where it is. I've marked it on the map." My pride was wounded. Maps have always been an interest of mine;

sometimes nearer an obsession.

The journey, of about ten miles, through a maze of sunken cow-dung caked lanes, was uneventful, if a little torturous.

"Damned French roads!" Howard observed. "I'm glad it's not my car being shaken to pieces." Howard's car, which was parked outside the notaire's, was a Range Rover and would have been easily equal to the task. Somehow, I rather doubted that he had ever engaged four-wheel drive, unless perhaps to park upon the pavement.

My own car, the Citroen, was used to this type of work, its 'sit-up-and-beg' hydraulic system having been originally designed to meet a specification that it should be able to take a farmer and his cargo of eggs over a ploughed field without breaking the eggs. Just the thing for the French countryside. You have merely to move a lever to take the undercarriage further off the road ('super-bounce' the kids call it). At it's highest setting, they say that you only need three wheels - but I've never tried that.

The property we were to visit was a smallholding at the end of a long and rutted track. Beyond the house there stretched an orchard of cider-apple trees which, at this end of season, were covered with small green fruit that made my mouth pucker just to look at them. Cows grazed peacefully under the trees. It was a typical Norman scene. I turned off the engine, got out of the car and breathed in deeply.

Howard looked around him suspiciously, seemingly unmoved by the beauty of the place. His eyes narrowed: "It's like something out of a horror movie. The peasants probably come after dark to make their sacrifices here. Druidical priests with sharp knives to cut out your heart. Look at those trees, just dripping with mistletoe." He was right. As is commonplace in such old orchards, great round balls of mistletoe hung in the low tree tops.

"Sacrificing virgins and pitchforking incomers!" He leered at Emma.

I'm not sure where Howard had come by his insight into French rural customs. Possibly he had seen a film of the storming of the Bastille on a double bill with 'Deliverance'.

"Er, yes," I said.

Feeling rather like a chatelaine, I took the great ring of keys that the notaire's assistant had given me, and turned to open the door. The first key didn't fit. Nor the second. Nor the third. Nor did any of the others. I was facing the estate agent's nightmare. **I had the wrong keys.** I rattled the door stupidly. It was still locked. There didn't seem an awful lot that I could do about it, for the whole place was shuttered up from the inside. "Damn." I muttered. Then, straightening up, I turned, taking care not to bump into Mr Avery, who had moved very close to me:

"I'm sorry, I seem to have been given the wrong keys."

"Here, give them me!" he snapped. Grabbing them from me, he tried them himself. Having satisfied himself that the reason that I had not opened the door was because I had the wrong keys, rather than because of my inability to use keys *per se*, he looked at me quizzically.

I gestured helplessly. "I'll have to ring the notaire to see whether the owner lives close by. There's a phone box in the village about a mile back." It seemed a long shot but it was worth a try.

"Get on with it then." Howard dismissed me sharply. "There's no saying you'll make it. You're taking enough risk driving a French car, but when you add a French telephone, there's no telling what might happen. We'll have a look around while you're away."

The overwhelming majority of my customers, regardless of their background or how much money they had, were very pleasant and likeable people. But, as my Auntie Vi used to say, 'there's always one'. I suspected that perhaps Howard was that one. Mrs Avery seemed used to coping with such situations. She followed me to my car, and, out of her husband's hearing, told me:

"I'm sorry that Howard's so abrupt. He's been under a lot of stress lately. You know how cut-and-thrust the City is."

I doubt whether he appreciated it, but Emma certainly was Howard's 'better half'. Completely disarmed by her few words, I drove off to make my phone call.

French or not, the telephone was working. When at last I got through, the notaire's assistant was very contrite. She was sorry, she had only started the job recently and had never visited the house. The keys must have been incorrectly labelled. "*Je suis desolé, Monsieur Bee-geen*, I don't have a telephone number for the owner, but his name is Monsieur Bigot and he lives at the mill."

I put the telephone back in its cradle and reached for the telephone directory - the *annuaire*. Damn! I had forgotten to ask which Commune M. Bigot lived in. Here was a further complication. The French work on such a local scale that if you want to think bigger than a Commune (parish) you can be in trouble.

Although an *annuaire* covers roughly the same number of subscribers as a British telephone directory, it does so by Commune, so all the people in St Anne are listed before all those in St Basil, who are listed before those in St Claire sur Origny, and so on and on. Which is fine if you happen to know that Monsieur Bigot lives in St Claire sur Origny, but not much use if you don't - and as St Claire sur Origny may only have 80 phones, there is no way you can wade through the whole book. I rang back at once. Engaged.

I stood in the booth for a long moment, pondering on what to do. Then I walked over to the bar across the road. The place was dark and smoky, even on this warm and sunny day. "Monsieur Bigot at *le moulin* you say?" Grunted the barkeeper. "He lives in St Etienne le Gros."

"Does he? *Merci, Monsieur.*" I dashed back to the telephone and thumbed through the directory to the entry for the commune of St Etienne le Gros. Bigot ....Bigot. That was an evocative name, though common enough in Normandy....was Monsieur Bigot a bigot? Where does the word 'bigot' come from anyway? Was it from some dyed-in-the-wool Norman of long ago, as 'Hooligan' comes from a badly behaved Irish family in the nineteenth century, or 'Boycott' from... well, I think that it was something to do with someone in Africa, although I can't remember what. ...and what had the original M. Bigot done to deserve that his name passed into the English language in such a pejorative way?

Putting the thought to the back of my mind, I rang the number. A pleasant voice answered. "*Allo, oui?*" (they always say that). I explained who I was and found that I was addressing Monsieur Bigot himself.

"*Le clé est sur le fut.*"

"The key is on the fire?" I repeated stupidly. It didn't sound right.

"*Non, pas le feu, le fut,*" the voice was amused, "*le tonneau ....la barrique.*"

"Ah, yes, I get it. Thank you, *Monsieur Bigot.*"

The key was on the barrel. I drove back to the farm, searched the outhouse and found the great iron museum-piece exactly where M. Bigot had told me it would be, hidden in an old bird's nest on top of one of those thousand-litre oak barrels which are so common in rural Normandy. I dusted the muck from my shirt, sending dust-motes in their millions into the sunlight, and smiled. All of my troubles were at an end.

....but where had my customers got to? With a quickening tread, I walked round the buildings, searching each of the barns, out-houses and dependencies. No luck. I called. No reply. The Averys had disappeared as if they had never been. Alien abduction? *Mais non*. This was France, not America.

The last place that I looked was in the orchard. Aha, what was the meaning of that! Some fifty or sixty metres from where I stood, the entire herd of cows were grouped round a tree, mooing crazily. Hot-footing it down the path as quickly as the cow-pats allowed, I solved the mystery of my disappearing customers. Stress, that great producer of adrenaline, had served Mr Avery well on this occasion. He had comfortably beaten his wife to the top of the tree.

"Get those bloody animals away from here!" he shouted down at me.

I looked at the milling animals with wonder, then studied the Averys more carefully. Emma was holding a large bunch of mistletoe. *Voilà le problème!* She had picked the mistletoe, which had caused the herd to chase her. I don't know what it is about mistletoe, but it drives cows to distraction.

Something similar had happened to me only the week before. David, barely five, and I, had picked the stuff in our neighbour's orchard. René's cows had come for us at the gallop. I had tried to shoo the beasts off by advancing on them arms wide apart - my usual method with cows - but they had not budged. Instead, they had jinked sideways and come at us again, butting at us to get at the mistletoe, until finally we had thrown it into a treetop (not knowing whether it would harm the cows), and beaten a hasty retreat.

"Looks like the Druids must have been listening, Mr Avery," I commented as I worked my way through the cows. "You must never mess with their mistletoe. Leave that in the tree and you'll be fine." Then I addressed Emma, (lapsing unconsciously - as I occasionally do in moments of stress - into my native Yorkshire): "There's nowt to worry about now, love. Let me help you down."

Reluctantly, she eased herself from the forked branches and lowered herself through my open arms. Howard scorned all assistance.

Mr Avery was not put into a good mood by all of this. He had nothing but criticism for the house (which was very good value). The plumbing was "bloody French jerry-built crap", the rooms were dirty and too big, the windows should have been double glazed. He had climbed up to the attic and been frightened by bats (I dread to think what they thought about him!). The state of the road leading up to the small holding was atrocious and the cow muck would make a mess of his Range Rover. I fancy Howard's ideal country retreat would have been in the Barbican Centre.

Emma looked long-suffering.

Howard's somewhat short temper finally burst when we got back to the notaire's office. It was just on one o'clock and the office would not reopen for another hour. Howard Avery wasn't used to wasting his time. He had gone off the idea of France altogether and was now considering buying a timeshare in the Florida Keys, where there was decent plumbing, the shops stayed open when you wanted them, the people almost spoke English, and there were no man-eating cows. Consequently he had no further use for me or the notaire.

Well, that was that. Some you win, some you lose - and sometimes, all unintentionally, you say just the wrong thing. It happens to all of us, I suppose. Those horrendous moments when you open your mouth and put your foot straight in.

My sally to Howard: "Well goodbye then, Mr Bigot", was something that was instinctive, unthinking, which could not be unsaid and which - were I to try for a million years - I would never persuade Mr Avery was not a deliberate insult. I could hardly blame him.

He regarded me with the utmost contempt, as if he perhaps believed that my sojourn in France had turned me into a 'frog' myself. He breathed-in sharply as if he was about to say something, then exhaled the air in an angry 'whoosh' and turned away without another word.

Emma winked at me.

I passed the next hour in my car, waiting for the notaire's *étude* to open. As usual on these occasions, I used the time to brush up on my French, using my patent French-learning 'card' method (which I will explain by-and-by).

I spent the rest of the afternoon with the notaire's assistant, a witty and intelligent woman in her twenties, who, while she didn't know her way round the notaire's properties much better than I did, was eager to help.

By the time that we had visited the two houses which we had already arranged to see (although, of course, without the Averys), drawn-up a timetable to see the dozen or so other properties on the notaire's books which interested me, and discussed ways and means of improving that good man's somewhat rudimentary system of dealing with property, it was time for me to go home.

Some people get their best ideas in the bath. I got mine while looking for an arrow which Alice had shot. I think, in another way, the arrow was fired by my builder friend, Mr Bignall.

We were intrepid archers, Alice, David and I. Alice was seven, David five and I was forty. As the biggest kid, I had the right to make the rules.

One of the great advantages of being in rural France is, of course, having room to breathe. Our great house, with an acre and a quarter of land, (larger than a football pitch) gave us much more scope for outside games than had our small English garden.

We could play hide and seek in the outhouses, hunt the grass snake in the orchard, or climb up the ladder into that strange loft on the back of the house, which was filled with bottles and odd wooden implements. The kids could cycle around the house (although the stones round the back made that a bit hard). But I suppose our favourite pastime was archery.

Making a bow is simple. You cut a bendy branch, thin and straight, slice notches at top and bottom, (a French *Opinel* knife is ideal for this) and feed in a piece of string. Arrows are not much harder. You just have to remember to make the flights or they won't fly straight.

At first we went for distance; who could fire from one end of the house to the other. Then we decided to try for height; could we clear the house? Here, we had to be very careful. Windows were involved - but French houses have a great advantage in this (admittedly rare) situation. They have shutters that are on the outside of the windows. True, outside shutters can be dangerous, as I have mentioned earlier, as you have to open the windows from the inside and lean quite a long way out to release them from their catches before you can close them. But they are essential for keeping in the warmth on a cold night; and of course, essential for archery practice.

It didn't take me long to close the shutters. All except for the attic. There were no shutters up there, so I just opened the window. Then the game commenced.

Alice, a good head taller than David, seemed to have the advantage, but her first shot merely hit the wall between the bottom and top windows.

"That's no good!" David rebuked his sister and drew back the drawstring. His arrow clattered against an upstairs shutter.

"Watch this then!" Alice, on her mettle now, notched another arrow to her bow, knelt down and aimed at a steeper angle. The arrow flew higher than David's. Up, up - and through the open attic window. There was an ominous crash.

"What have you done, child?"

We tore through the front door, across the tiled living room, up the uncarpeted stair, and to the door to the attic. Beyond the door, a small stair led to the great open space that stretched the length of the house. It was gloomy up there. It was, like most attics, full to the brim with treasures, or junk, which had made the move with us and sat there undisturbed ever since.

The crash had been a pudding bowl, standing partly unwrapped near the open window. An old plain white bowl, much crazed, which Ann had used for Christmas puddings. Not any more she wouldn't. The arrow was among the shards. I carefully picked up the pieces and glanced incuriously at the box on which the bowl had stood. It was marked 'Alan's stuff' and, in my handwriting, *'Culture Shock'*.

"Daddy," said Alice with all the authority of her seven summers. "I think we've had enough of these dangerous games. I think we need to calm down now. Let's play the 'everything game'."

"Come on dad!" agreed David.

The 'everything game' was more of an occupation for a rainy day or the winter than a nice warm day like this, but I was outvoted. It consists (or consisted, they're a little old for it now) of getting out every single one of the kids' toys; cars, boats, dolls, bricks, soldiers, teddies and so on, and making a continuous story of them that spread across the whole of the upstairs.

For instance, boats would be in the bath. On the floor next to the bath might be an airfield. Next to the airfield, a road made of wooden bricks, crowded with cars, would lead to another room where the cuddly toys were having tea. And so on, and on, and on. It was an absorbing game, but not one that Ann was terribly keen on; which is why we usually played it in her absence.

My mind wasn't really on the 'everything game' though. My mind was on *Culture Shock*. It was a novel which I'd written when I was in my twenties. It was set in North Wales in the 'sixties and concerned a religious cult which was led by a manipulative 'guru' whose real objectives were more financial and sexual than religious. I wrote it a long time before Waco, and Guyana, and all those other cult scandals. I must have been psychic. I had never found a publisher for it.

What was it Mr Bignall had said? "You ought to write a book of all this." Could I write another book? I had a lot of raw material already, mostly in one of the very rooms in which we were playing the 'everything game'; the spare bedroom, now my workroom.

I had been writing for years. Mostly user guides for the computer systems that I had designed or written. Nothing there to thrill a maiden's heart, but at least I knew that I could lay out my ideas in a sensible and understandable progression, which, while not romantic, is as necessary to a piece of writing as decent foundations are to a house. But as well as foundations, I would need materials!

Part of my material could be the stuff which I had written for my customers. Guides about various aspects of French life, such as learning the language, the buying process, education and a dozen other things besides. The guides were my way of avoiding repeatedly answering the same questions, and, as I've said, an attempt to provide 'service plus' to justify the very high agency charges.

Besides these mini 'Biggins guides to living and working in France', I was also bashing out essay after essay for my exams. I was studying for a degree-level qualification, the Diploma of the Institute of Linguists, for which there are no set books and no classroom sessions (I think there are classes in the U.K, but you don't have to attend them to take the exams). This absence of a formal structure is very helpful in that it allows you to study in your own way in your own time. But to get up to the necessary high level, you still need to put in the work.

In order to get the Diploma, you need to pass four exams (modules) which you choose out of a possible six. I had taken four already and failed one of them. In order to retake that exam, I was constantly revising - which meant translating articles from the French press into English. The topics that I was covering were many and sometimes bewildering, economics, history, tourism, language and humour, (always the hardest) among others. I also had a pile of essays which I had written for exams that I had already passed.

Then there was the wildlife of Normandy, and its history; subjects which interested me and which I knew a bit about.

Perhaps more important than any of this was what lay in my head. The stories of the people whom I had met, small farmers and their lifestyles, their philosophy, their diet, their memories. And of course there were the English property buyers. I had met some fascinating people.

Naturally I would need to treat people with care. I would have to get permission to portray some events, apply a little camouflage to one or two. Whereas it wouldn't matter at all if Mr Bignall was recognised, it would not do for Howard to be. Mine was a privileged position, I must not abuse it.

I had a great mass of material to hand; some of it wonderful and rich and exotic; but was I a good enough artist to make a decent book from it? If I could, I had no doubt it would find an audience. Rural France is a subject dear to the heart of a good proportion of the English population.

How would I go about it? It wouldn't be like the 'everything game'. I would need to discard a lot more than I kept. That would probably be difficult in itself, if our attic full of junk was anything to go by.

.... The first question I must answer, before I sat down to write, was what kind of book it was to be. I didn't want to write a guide to buying French property. I wanted something alive. Something full of anecdote and speech and humour. Something which would inform the reader, but delight him (or her) as well. Something to express my love of this area and its people. Something as individual to me as my own fingerprint.

"Come on dad. Concentrate please! Get the windmill down from the top of my cupboard!"
.... and something that included a little of the wonders and mysteries of my own small universe.

Quite a challenge. Was I up to it?

SELLING FRENCH DREAMS

Wordsmithing. Repointing.
At the Depot de Vente.
The art of Monsieur Fouchard. Percy dump.

Alchemy. n. medieval forerunner of chemistry,
especially pursuit of transmutation of baser metals
into gold or silver.
        (The concise Oxford dictionary)

One of the few things that I can remember my chemistry
teacher telling me, is that it is possible nowadays to change
one metal into another. He even told me roughly how to do it.
But it was all over my head. Apparently it is so costly as to be
uneconomic.
    Writing, turning thoughts, memories and facts into a
quicksilver that runs across the page, drawing the eye with it,

sparkling, running and twisting with a life of its own, generally involves the burning of much midnight oil. Often, it too is uneconomic.

I suppose that writing isn't quite alchemy though. The raw ingredients must be more than base metal. Perhaps it's more like panning for gold.

Then, when you've got your gold, or your story, you've got to fashion and refine it, or, no matter what lies beneath the surface, it will just seem heavy and dull. In book terms, the story of an amazing life can be told in such a way as to make the reader nod over the pages.

The trouble with this business of word-smithing, of course, is that the raw materials are rarely visible. You sit at your desk and stare blankly at the word processor (or, if you are less technologically advanced, at the typewriter - a very much tougher proposition - cutting and pasting is seamless on a computer; when done physically it can be very messy).

You then find that:

i). You don't know what to say, or:

ii). There is a matter of pressing urgency that you had forgotten all about until now. Typically this will be:

You need a cup of tea.

The pencil needs sharpening. However, one of the kids has pinched the pencil sharpener (maybe the same one who removed both pairs of scissors, the ruler and paper glue). You detour into her bedroom to look for it, only to find that the bin is overflowing and needs emptying. While picking up the bin, you come across her school report book and become engrossed with the fact that she isn't doing very well at art.

So you decide to go up into the attic to find a nineteen seventies part-work on the Impressionists that you're pretty sure that you haven't thrown away. While up there you find your grandfather's cigarette cards from the thirties, and spend a profitable couple of hours studying the flags of a world long since gone.

The post arrives. It includes a bank statement. You spend several hours in catatonic shock.

The chair sellers arrive. (If in England, please substitute a phone call from a double-glazing salesperson.) The chair seller is as constant in rural France as hay fever, and as difficult to shake off. If you don't buy from him, he'll keep trying. If you do buy, you can be guaranteed follow up sale calls for all eternity (trying to wear you down, until you utter the magic phrase: 'yes, I'll take a standing order for two chairs a month until I die - oh, and if you like, I'll stipulate in my will that the kids have to continue the contract in order to inherit').

The dog walks up to you and stretches meaningfully, filling you with guilt and leading you out for a walk.

The cat sits on your lap.

A number of these things happen at once.

Somehow you overcome these obstacles and pan for golden thoughts and memories, refine them, polish them, set them, test them, store them away with a grim smile and move on to your next nugget ....but first you take a quick look at what you've just written.

A terrible shock! The three pages you have wrestled from the cosmos turn out not to be gold after all. Some villain's been meddling! Instead of the light, witty essay or the profound and moving passage that you thought that you'd written, you find - fool's gold - a pile of dross!

"It smells of poo."

I am disturbed from my reverie. Was it a call from inside my own head? Revision number whatever-it-was hadn't been very satisfactory it was true - but poo?

"It smells of poo." The call comes again. It is real. It is David and he is calling from downstairs.

"What is it darling?"

"It smells of poo." He is slightly truculent at having to repeat himself so often. "And it's coming from round the back of the house."

He leads me round the back. Phew! He's right. A very nasty niff is coming from the stones. "Thanks son. I'll have a look. Could you ask your mum to come out?"

He leaves me. Moments later, Ann arrives.

"It's those builders," she says, putting a hanky to her nose. "They've broken the pipe to the septic tank."

'Those builders' were Alf and George, who had just repointed the back of the house.

I suppose that our house was built around a hundred years ago, but that's purely a guess. There's no way that I know of to date these Norman stone houses, unless it is through title deeds. The traditional style continues in use.

At some time before we bought it, the front of the house had been completely repointed, but the back had been ignored. The back of the house is a great long wall, punctured only by two tiny windows. Here, the mortar had corroded and dropped out in many places to make a haven for small creatures in the winter. Earlier in the year, we had heard all sorts of scurryings and scamperings from inside the wall. I even suspected that the Russian hamsters that had mysteriously disappeared might be living there, if they hadn't been eaten by the cats.

At any rate, we had decided to have it repointed before the various creatures took up winter quarters in it.

42

Being in the estate agency business, there is never a problem finding workmen. They make a beeline for you. As I've mentioned, Dick had compiled a register of such artisans - both English and French (and a blacklist too, but that's another story). For this job, I chose Alf and George, a couple of guys who were doing up a property that they had bought, and who were always on the lookout for a bit of paid work. They were happy to do the pointing, and one or two other bits and pieces.

They brought their scaffolding, drove round the back of the house, mixed up the mortar and got on with it. It had taken them four days to do the job. An excellent job too. They had left yesterday.

Between us, we worked out what must have happened. The house is surrounded by a driveway. Round the front and at the side, where we parked the cars, it is made of fine gravel. At the rear, however, the stones are very much larger and we never drove on that area.

Upon close inspection, the area that the smell was coming from was in a very slight dip. That dip was directly in line with the downstairs and upstairs toilets (the one being directly above the other).

That seemed partially to explain a mystery that I ought to have solved as soon as we moved in. The house, as is normal in the French countryside, is not on mains drainage but uses a septic tank. I had never known where that tank was. I had assumed that it was in or behind the orchard at the back of the house, but the two or three times when I'd had a look for it, I had discovered nothing. Now it looked as though we had at least found the trench which led to it. Alf and George's Transit van must have been too heavy and fractured it.

Ann and I looked at each other in silence. Here was a pretty pickle.

The next thing was to find someone to fix the mess. British builders might be available quickly enough, but getting a French artisan (and the repair and emptying of the fosse would need such an expert) to do anything quickly is not easy. The best that we could do was a promise from a Monsieur Fouchard that he would arrive in four days.

In the meantime, of course, we had to put the toilets out of bounds. With our family of four, it promised to be a tricky few days. We couldn't very well bother our neighbours René or Albert every time we wanted to use the loo, so we had to find an alternative means of waste disposal. We decided to visit the *Depot de Vente* in Villedieu to search for suitable receptacles.

The *Depot de Vente* is a rather fine institution. Here, anyone who wants to sell anything can take it along, price it up and leave it. If it sells, the vendor pays the owner of the *Depot de Vente* a cut - perhaps twenty percent. If it hasn't sold after a certain time, the owner of the *Depot* will ask the vendor to remove it. In a rural *Depot*, one can always expect a wide selection of items. Many of them are, of course, absolute rubbish. Knackered lamps, raffia wine bottle holders, mildewed oil paintings of white horses in the surf, busts of the dreaded *Général*, that sort of tat.

But often there is treasure too. Unconsidered trifles such as old wooden benches, the odd bit of debris from the war - a German helmet or two, a jerrycan, perhaps a stengun. Some interesting crockery. We found what we wanted. Three chamberpots.

We also got a toy tank for David. In England, metal toy tanks seem to have been removed from normal circulation and passed into the realms of 'military modelling' (as if that in itself was anything but a form of playing) at ludicrous expense. So

David, with his Solido AMX-30T, had a toy denied to his contemporaries in England.

Ann got a flower vase in the form of a crowing cock in striking reds and greens. It has that superb French vulgarity that is somehow loveable - unless you see it too early in the morning.

For the next few days I acted as chamber pot emptier.

When finally he arrived, Monsieur Fouchard was a small, dapper man with a tobacco-stained moustache. He looked a little like Marshal Foche, the great First World War French general. We shook hands and, rather as the Marshal might have conferred a medal, he presented me with a somewhat grimy business card:

N. Fouchard,
Expert in septic tanks and drainage services.
Small digger available.

Alice and I took him round the back and explained what had happened and that we needed the fractured pipe removed and replaced. As we didn't know where the septic tank itself was located, we would be grateful if he could find it and empty it. It was as if Monsieur Fouchard had been wound up and released. His moustache seemed to quiver as he spoke:

"The installation of a *fosse septique* and its ancilliary piping and culverting must initially be the object of a specific request at the Mairie in order to evaluate its impact on the environment. The description of the works is to be accompanied by a plan of the ancillary piping and trenching, along with any neighbouring wells and water courses."

"Yes, but...."

"For a private house the cistern must be two cubic metres

and the trench twenty-four metres long. The drainage pipes must be lain in a trench at least fifty centimetres deep. But one should be aware that even at this depth the position of the pipe is visible from the surface...."

"Not on gravel it isn't," I broke in. But Monsieur Fouchard was well into his stride. He held up a hand, palm outward:

"Because, Monsieur, the grass always grows a little greener above it. Another problem is ventilation. The installation should have two kinds of ventilation, which may not smell too sweetly. So it's best to put it as far from the house as possible, and mask it if possible with shrubs or roses..."

I interrupted his monologue. "Yes, yes, that's all very interesting Mr Fouchard. But to be honest, we don't really need the basic principles of the *fosse*. What we need is to have this pipe replaced and to know where the main tank is so that it can be drained."

Monsieur Fouchard's moustache definitely had quivered this time. He carried on majestically. "Also make sure that you do not plant large trees near the pipe work, because of their roots. You musn't skimp on the length of the pipes; and you should place the main tank where it will be of the least inconvenience. Unless you're a fan of pickaxe and spade, the installation of the *fosse* and pipework should be carried out by a trained man, with a digger of his own."

I was caught between irritation and amusement by now. The fellow sounded like a promotional brochure. I tried to get him back on track. "A digger such as your own, no doubt? Most impressive. It should make it a fairly quick job to dig out our trench and replace the broken pipe."

"One moment, if you please, *Monsieur Bee-geen*. We will come to that in good time. I have yet to explain the *Puit Perdu*."

"The lost well? We haven't lost the well. It's the septic tank that we can't find."

He tutted me to silence. "Not at all the same thing. The *puit perdu* is not a well which has been lost. It is a hole dug into the ground and filled with coarse gravel. It is to drain away the water which falls on your roof. The volume of the hole depends on the size of your roof and the *région* in which you live. Here in Normandy, for example, you would need a hole of two cubic metres for eighty square metres of roof. Given the amount of work this represents, and the transport of the gravel, one is always well advised to entrust a task of that nature to a specialist enterprise, which has it's own digger...."

By this time Alice and I had 'lost it.' We were totally convulsed and could not have interrupted if we'd tried. However, Monsieur Fouchard had finished his lecture. Gradually his eyes lost their far-away look and focussed on us. I tried to compose my face, but it wasn't easy. Alice didn't help. For a moment I thought that Monsieur Fouchard had realised that we were laughing at him. Probably I was mistaken, for the flicker of annoyance that I thought I saw was gone before I was sure that it was there at all. He was talking again:

"*Eh, oui*, I think that I can replace the pipe easily enough. I think that I am also going to be of help in tracing the course of the pipe after it leaves the gravelled area, and hence the location of your *fosse septique*. Do you have, perhaps, *Monsieur Bee-geen*, a shoe?"

"A shoe?" Was it his turn to make fun of me?

"A shoe. A thing that one puts on a foot. And what is more, a shoe with a shoelace."

"Of course I have a shoe, but I don't see...."

"....of course an old fashioned fob watch with a chain would be better."

"A fob watch?"

"Yes, a fob watch would be wisest. I could of course dig under your orchard to find the tank, but I don't think that would be advisable. For one thing, it would disturb the roots and possibly kill some of your excellent apple trees, which I note are dripping with fruit. Then again, it would be a long-winded and costly affair."

I looked at the orchard. There was no doubt that what he said was true. The apples were about ready for picking. There was a good crop which, as I had explained to 'Monsieur Pomme', I intended to sell to the local co-operative for cider making. I certainly didn't want them disturbed if it could be helped. "A fob watch?"

"Just so, a fob watch." Monsieur Fouchard seemed to be getting a little impatient. "But as I'm sure that you have no such thing, a shoe will suffice. As long as it is laced."

I thought for a moment. I did, as a matter of fact, have a fob watch. I had bought it for fifteen shillings in Norwich many years ago. A fine watch, an Ingersoll, which still ticked away as well as ever, but unfortunately the hands had fallen off. No harm could come to it, but... "And what do you intend to do with this shoe, or watch if you prefer?"

"Ah, *Monsieur Bee-geen*, I do prefer. What do I intend to do? Why, God willing, find the course of your drainage trench, and hence deduce the location of your septic tank."

"How?"

"How? Why by the art of dowsing. There is a gift of God which is given to some men which bestows on them the ability to trace water, or streams, or even drainage trenches. Not every man possesses this art, though more than you might believe."

I smiled. More than I might believe? As I doubted whether any man possessed the art, I was sure that he was right.

Perhaps he saw my doubt, for his impatience returned: "The watch then. But if I am successful, then I will claim my reward."

"Which is?"

"Let me see." He mused a moment. "In order that you understand the advantages that you will gain from our bargain, I will enumerate them. You will not have an orchard of uprooted trees. Nor will you need to pay for the long use of my jolly little digger and the relaying of your pipe. These are not trivial things, I am sure that you agree. I, for my part, will claim little. Let us say merely a couple of sacks of your apples, and that you will remove the rubbish that I generate. Not the contents of the septic tank of course. I shall dispose of that. However, I am bound to make a bit of mess. The old pipe for instance. I am sure that you can take that away."

The offer sounded a little malodorous but perfectly feasible. It was only a couple of miles to the tip at Percy and if the piping was bagged up, it should not be too big a job. Perhaps I could borrow Ann's estate car... "Fine." I agreed. "*D'accord*. I will find my watch." I glanced at Alice and smiled. This should be good for an anecdote at least. She, however, looked perfectly serious and trusting. Ah the innocence of children!

I found the watch surprisingly easily. Mr Fouchard took it and weighed it quizzically on the gnarled palm of his left hand. He looked at me as if I was making fun of him: "*Il faut avoir un lacet.*" Of course, the chain being long gone, he needed something to dangle it from. A shoelace. Sheepishly, I took one from my shoe. Slowly but methodically, he tied it on. Then he went to the edge of the gravel.

He stood for a time until the watch hung unmoving from his hand. I looked closely. I also studied the soil in the orchard. The line of a pipe might have shown beneath a clean green lawn but it did not show here, amid the teasels and nettles and docks that choked the ground. The watch did not move. I raised an eyebrow at Monsieur Fouchard. "*Il faut attendre.*" He grunted.

So we waited. Slowly, almost imperceptibly, the watch began to move. Then it jerked off to the right. Monsieur Fouchard grunted. "Promising. Yes, quite promising. Would you like to give it a try?"

I took the watch gingerly and let it hang down. Nothing happened. I waited. Still nothing.

"Oh well. And then?" The grizzled contractor gently took the watch from me. More quickly this time, it began to move, to jerk. He took a pace to the right. It spun on itself, straight down. He took a pace forward. It jerked to the right again. Quite without wanting to, I realised that I was jerking my head from side to side as well. "A bit deep this one," he said with professional satisfaction. "Well laid."

And so, little by little, we progressed at a thirty degree angle across the orchard. I felt surprisingly clumsy and vulnerable being down to only one shoelace. I moved with all the grace and presence of a black-suited stork. Finally, we left the trees. We were near to the boundary of our property, right by the edge of the wood stack.

"Perhaps you would remove some of this wood, *Monsieur Bee-geen.*"

"But I'm in my suit." I grumbled.

"I'll hold your jacket, dad." Offered Alice.

Thanks, girl. So I took off my jacket, rolled up my sleeves and, trying not to soil my clothes, did as I was bid. It was no easy task, for the long props were laid hither and thither across each other and covered with brambles. Finally I had cleared a space.

"A spade perhaps?"

I opened my mouth. M. Fouchard raised an eyebrow and I closed it again. The time to protest - if there had ever been a time to protest - was over. Somewhere along the line - although when and how I couldn't say - Monsieur Fouchard had achieved moral ascendancy. He knew it, I knew it, and he knew that I knew it. I fetched the spade.

"Could you dig a little?"

So, feeling more of a fool than ever, I dug. At a short depth, the metal rang on something solid. Clearing away the muck, I came to a piece of concrete. Clearing more dirt revealed a lid.

"*Eh voila. La fosse.*"

To say that I was surprised would be understating things.

Monsieur Fouchard laid a new piece of pipe. That afternoon he returned with a suction cleaner and emptied the tank. "Very full," was his verdict, "perhaps next time you will call me sooner, *Monsieur Bee-geen*." He shrugged his shoulders. "And, who knows, perhaps next time you will have a little more faith."

I shook hands with him gingerly and he left with my payment and a great number of apples.

My wife was surprisingly unsympathetic to my request that I borrow her car to take the detritus to the dump: "But while you're at it, there are three black bags waiting to go."

As there is no refuse collection in rural Percy, I had to take all our rubbish to the tip, which made us a little more prudent about creating so much of it. We composted everything that we could (Of course, a large garden helped somewhat in this respect.)

So I folded down the back seats of my faithful Citroen, packed the rubbish up very carefully and loaded the car. It was always a pleasure to take one of the kids with me on these excursions, and this time David volunteered to accompany his dad. "Can we take Flavie?"

"I suppose so." I eyed the pesky pup.

Percy rubbish dump is situated in a fairly remote part of the Commune and is not well sign-posted (I suppose it doesn't want to attract out-of-town rubbish). It had taken me a while to track it down.

"It's on the road to Montpertuis, you can't miss it." I had been told more than once. One lesson that I had learnt from selling property is that when you are told 'you can't miss it', a place is going to be very difficult to find. But by now my old car knew its way.

A rubbish dump is a profoundly significant thing. It tells us an awful lot about our society. Somebody should write a thesis on it: 'A comparative study of European tips'.

An English tip, for example, would reveal everything about England because just about everything eventually ends up there. Our tips are crammed with useful things; not that the people who leave them want them to go to waste. You can tell that by the way that they religiously separate out those things which can be recycled.

I am frequently amazed by English tips. In my irregular trips, apart from the usual mounds of washing machines, fridges, hoovers, bicycles and the like, I've also spotted antiques, a box of wigs, a mannequin and piles of books and records. A tip in a rich area is undoubtedly more rewarding than a jumble sale in a poor one. That is a very disturbing thought.

In Holland, I believe, the people leave things that they don't want, but which are still serviceable, out on the street on a designated day of the week. If anybody else wants them, they simply take them. Anything not taken is cleared up the next day by the bin men.

But I reckon rural French tips must be the poorest in the West. Percy tip had little of interest. Anything that was there had long outlived any value whatsoever. It was with little sense of wanting to prolong the occasion, then, that I hauled the black bags out of the car and flung them into the skip.

Percy tip differs from its English counterparts also in that safety is not such a prominent feature. Again this is a commonplace in rural France.

In the case of Percy dump, the skip was buried into the earth so that the lip was flush with the ground. I always made sure that the kids' were well away from the edge. But I had counted without Flavie. After I threw the bags into the empty container, in an excess of canine zeal, she jumped in after them. The consequence was that she was eight feet below ground level. Fortunately, the next visitor to the tip had a ladder with him, so I managed to rescue the dirty but unharmed dog.

When we got home, I was bawled out by Ann. (It was my fault her mutt had leaped into a hole?) and told to get across to René's to get some milk. Clutching the *pot au lait* and my grievance, I made my way to the milking parlour. René was doing the milking. He put a milking cup on the udder of a cow. The pump thudded rhythmically away and the milk spurted up through the rubber pipe and into a churn. My farmer friend seemed in a bit of subdued mood; he had mislaid some official form, and wasn't looking forward to the possible repercussions.

He filled the milk can and grumbled briefly about officialdom. We shook hands and I walked home.

My mind was bubbling with the wonderful events of the day; the shoelace, the magic of the swinging fob watch, the clang of the spade on concrete. In a mood of self-righteousness, and influenced no doubt by René's experience, I decided that now was the time to file the receipt which Monsieur Fouchard had given me.

It wasn't that difficult. The previous owner of our house has left a steel filing cabinet and quite a few papers relating to the place, and Ann had used this as the basis for our own filing system. I opened the drawer marked 'House and Car'. My wife had been very efficient. There were compartments for telephone bills, electricity bills - even, I was surprised to see, one marked *'fosse septique'*. At the bottom of the cardboard sleeve lay a rather dog-eared piece of paper. Gingerly, I took it out to study. It was an eighteen month old receipt for the installation of a septic tank - our septic tank. A business card was clipped to it, the writing all but obscured by a great earthy thumbprint. I had no difficulty in reading it though:

N. Fouchard,
Expert in septic tanks and drainage services.
Small digger available.

MOUNT ORGUEIL JERSEY

The Jersey lass. The Channel Islands.
Jersey and a new start. The Occupation Hospital.

Our house is full of references to the sea, from the carved tern on the mantelpiece to the puffin in the stairwell and the pictures of trawlers in the living room.

Even the hall, stairs and landing share in the theme. In the downstairs hall, on the bottom part of the wall is painted an underwater sea-scene, dark, with deep water fishes swimming there. Gradually, as the wall rises, the sea gets lighter and bluer, until halfway up the stairs a dolphin leaps above the surface. Then we are into land and air, culminating on the ceiling where there are fluffy clouds, the sun and birds. (I'm keeping my eyes open for three plaster ducks to fly up the wall but I haven't had any luck yet).

Although this maritime flavour is more Ann's doing than anyone else's, all of the family are rather partial to a good beach. Our favourite Norman beach is not far north of Granville and is quiet even by French standards. It is approached by the *Route Submersible* which, as its name suggests, disappears beneath the waves at (very) high tides. This road crosses a salt-marsh about a thousand yards wide, at its mid-point crossing a stream which is a trickle at low tide. This creek, belonging sometimes to the land, sometimes to the sea, is an added reason for visiting the beach.

When the children were small, we would often go there. Gumboots on, the four of us would wade in and out of the maze of waterways that thread through the salt marshes (*les salines*) among the camphor banks and the sea holly, looking into and wading through the pools. Crabs were our normal catch. These we would collect in a bucket until it was time to go, when we would release the poor, mystified creatures back into a pool.

Then we would go onto the beach.

The astonishing width of the Norman beaches, here at least a mile and a half wide at low tide, means that the slope is very gradual to the sea and swimming is safe, although preferably on a rising tide (on a couple of occasions I have been swept along the foreshore, quite powerless on a falling tide. It is not an experience that I would want to repeat). Luckily the beach is patrolled in summer.

When not in the sea, we would walk beside it, picking up cuttlefish or popping bladderwrack (*varech* in French) or, if we were lucky enough to find some flat stones, playing Ducks and Drakes. Flavie also loved these outings.

Of course, the sea is of interest to a wider audience than the

Biggins family. Houses near the coast command a premium. The nearer to the sea, the greater the premium. In Normandy, the French, by-and-large, have little interest in the old, sometimes tumble-down, rural properties which interest the English. By the seaside, it is another matter.

It was by the seaside, in a village north of Avranches, that I met the Nicholls, one of the nicest English couples that I met in Normandy.

The encounter came, as with many another in Normandy, because of a request to value their property. The Nicholls ran a small restaurant, which I will call 'The Jersey Lass'.

The restaurant was situated in a village which is popular with families. The beach isn't particularly good there, being mud rather than sand, but the settlement has a homely and pleasantly old-fashioned feel, with small shops selling nets, swimming trunks, water wings, plastic boats, sea-shell boxes and a host of such wonderful seaside knick-knackery.

The short summer season was over when I visited, and the houses were mostly shuttered up. Walking along a deserted street, I had the strange experience of being hailed by a Frenchman who mistook me for his son.

The restaurant was a narrow and tall building in a road near to the sea and it was Beryl Nicholls who answered the door.

"We've just closed," she said, pointing at the *Fermé* sign on the door.

I explained who I was, and she opened the door wider and ushered me in. I told her that I was particularly interested in 'The Jersey Lass', as many British visitors were on the look-out for premises where they could live and also make a little money, whether it be by camping, bed and breakfast or, as in this case, as a restaurant.

Beryl was a short English woman in her fifties of great

vitality; a little like Beryl Reed in fact. She had the stamp of 'organiser' written all over her. She cleared some plates and cups from a table and gestured to me to sit down. I took my place and put my clipboard on the table.

A clipboard is an essential piece of the estate agent's armoury. In fact it's ideal camouflage in most situations. I have walked round factories, offices, military installations and indeed Parliament itself with my clipboard and only once been challenged. Carrying a clipboard *and an apple* I have never been challenged.

"Well young man," (I warmed to Beryl already), "let's get down to business. The Jersey Lass is a very popular place. We have lots of English customers and lots of French too. Bill and I have had many happy years here, and it's only the fact that we want to retire that is making us sell."

"Yes, that's interesting." I muttered, making notes.

"Let me show you around," she said, slightly impatiently. "I'm sorry to have to rush you, but we don't close for long in the afternoons. I'm opening up again in an hour and I've still got the washing up to do."

"Yes," her words poured out as she bustled me upstairs, "we're very popular. My lad Derek speaks French - he should do, he went to school here - and Bill - my husband, you'll meet him in a minute - and I can get by in the language. We're very popular with English visitors in summer, and with the French all the year round. They do love a Devon cream tea." She paused to take breath, then she was off again:

"We close on Monday. Tuesday we have Monsieur and Madame Moncet, he's the Mayor. Wednesday we have the Anglo-French society to practice their language - there's quite a thriving club here you know - Thursday we get the singers - my Bill plays the saxophone and I'm a singer - Friday's the bridge club. The weekend of course we get the weekenders. They come down here in and out of season. It's so mild you see; and from up top you can see Mont St Michel. Did you notice that?"

"Er, yes." I replied a little distractedly as I measured the room.

"Course you did. Good lad. Now this in here is the upstairs dining room. Eighteen covers and very popular. See the paintings on the wall? Local artists. Very popular with painters, is the bay."

I looked at the mass of watercolours of the bay, Mont St Michel, and boats, and vowed inwardly to keep Ann away from 'The Jersey Lass'.

"Come on upstairs Alan. Mind the Grandfather." This was not an allusion to an aged relative, but to the large clock that was on a half-landing, and which had to be squeezed past to get into the private quarters.

"We've two bedrooms, a lounge, a kitchen, a bathroom and a veranda up here. This here's the lounge. And this here's my Bill."

Bill stood up. He was a slightly dark man perhaps sixty years old, with a nice smile and a hatching of laughter lines around his eyes. He was in his dressing gown. There was something slightly bohemian about him, as you'd expect - or at least strongly hope for - in a saxophone player.

"This is Alan from the estate agency."

"We'll forgive you that."

"I should hope so!" said Beryl in mock surprise. "He's going to sell our house for us!"

"Come on Alan, hate to hurry you. This is the veranda. Lovely sunny aspect. That's why there are so many cacti up here. That and the fact that they don't take a lot of looking after.

Gets the sun all afternoon, doesn't it Bill?" She didn't wait for an answer, but was off again. "That's Joey the parrot. West African. Got a bit of a tongue on him I'm afraid. That's Bill that's taught him that!"

In a torrent, Beryl told me her life story. It was rich and steamy in parts. She was a Jersey girl (hence the name of the restaurant) who had sung in many parts of the world.

I told her that I would be visiting Jersey in a couple of days time, for a property show. "You'll do well there," she commented, "there's lots of money over there; and those that can't afford the fancy prices on the island quite often buy a holiday home over here."

She had met up with Bill half a lifetime ago and the two had never been apart since. They had settled in Normandy quite a few years back; dividing their time between the restaurant, the upbringing of their son Derek (who I was to meet later and who was as engaging as his parents) and travelling around the world to sing.

The restaurant had become the focal point of the artistic life of the French seaside village. Quite a few of the English community in Normandy are musicians or singers. Their number is, I think, probably only exceeded by small builders. There is definitely happiness in music, for, although they must have the same basic worries as anyone else, the musicians whom I met seemed somehow happier than other people.

Maybe there's nothing surprising in that, for I don't suppose that there is anything in this world of man that gives more delight than music. Nevertheless, I had not noticed or considered it before. One of the chief rewards of being an estate agent is that you are privileged to look for a moment into some of those other 'ponds' of human existence of which you are hardly aware and wonder and learn from what is in them.

"Come on, have to hurry you. Look," Beryl considered a second, "I'll just show you the garden and then I must get on. I'm not being rude. If you need any more time to measure up, or have any more questions, I'll get Bill down. You might find him a bit dozy though, he's not at his brightest first thing. Poor fellow has just woken up. We had the Mayor round last night and it turned into a bit of a session. I don't think the old chap's up to it any more."

I didn't know whether 'the old chap' was Bill or the Mayor; but I could see that it might be hard to keep up with Beryl.

"Here we are then. Our menagerie. Could you put this in the details? It would be nice if we could get someone to take it over. In fact it would be more than nice. It's very important." She looked at me intently. "Do you think you might find someone willing to take them over?"

I looked at the cages, sheds and hutches that took up the rear end of the plot (beyond the tea garden). There must have been more than a dozen of them. "What do you keep?"

"Well, it's mostly what we've been given really. We're a bit of a soft touch. Joey you know about, then there's the rabbits, the cats, the dog, the chickens, the bantams, doves, weasels - oh and the grass snake - we'll release him soon I hope - and the stoat. But the rarest, and the biggest trouble as well, is this fellow." She pointed to a wire fronted cage. I looked in with interest but was disappointed to see nothing more than a sleeping cat. Beryl noted my look and nudged me:

"Look at his tail."

I did as I was told. "And? It's just a tail isn't it? Except that it seems to have a couple of rings on it."

"Which is what makes him a wild cat. Derek got him when he was driving back from Spain. He stopped at a bar and was given this injured cat. I don't know what marks us Nicholls out

61

as suckers, but if there's a creature in trouble, one way or another it'll end up here. He's the devil to look after; but I'm hoping he'll be better soon and we can take him back down south." She looked at me again.

"Alan, you do think it will be possible to find someone who will keep the animals? I don't want to think of harm coming to them. We won't have room for them where we're going."

Of course, I could not say who might be interested in buying the property; but I said that it was the kind of place that would attract people like herself and Bill; cosmopolitan, bohemian, friendly people. Nice people. For such people, the animals would probably be an added attraction. And I meant it.

She brightened on the instant. "I do hope so; and thank you for cheering me up. Come on, time to open. Have a cup of tea."

As we walked back up the garden, that occupational hazard of the open air manifested itself. Suddenly, across the notes that I was writing, in the centre of my clipboard, a white spatter of bird muck appeared.

"That's typical." Beryl commented. "Create a paradise for wildlife and they just dump all over you!"

I sat drinking my tea as Beryl opened up the restaurant. Two French ladies were already on the step and waiting. Beryl ushered them in, speaking briefly to them as she did so, evidently concerning me.

One of them came over to me and, smiling, wagged a finger. "*Monsieur vous ne devez pas absolument vendre cette maison.*" (Sir, you must on no account sell this house).

As I drove back, I reflected with what ease Beryl and Bill, broken-French notwithstanding, had integrated into society here. How different a story was theirs than that which I had heard so often from English people who felt alone and isolated from the life of the community around them. In part, of course, it was the ready-made meeting place that was their business. In part I think it was the greater sociability of their small town than the country. In part I think it was the universal language, music.

As The Jersey Lass had remarked, buying a house in Normandy is often an attractive idea for people from her island, as the journey between the two takes less than an hour.

My own trip, for the property show, started from the port of Granville. A fast, bucketing, boat took me across to the island. I had been looking forward to the trip. I'd always wanted to visit the Channel Islands, although I could have wished to do so on a calmer day. A stiff breeze was blowing and by the time we were out to sea, the waves were choppy and steep. As excited as a child, I braced my legs and looked through the spray towards Jersey.

The Channel Islands are in many ways a bit of a British anomaly. They don't appear on British Ordnance survey maps for a start, but they do on French ones. However, as they lie only a few miles from the French coast, and are clearly visible from it, but sixty and more miles from England, that makes perfect sense geographically.

Culturally too, the islands' history lies with the French mainland. They are plastered with French place names and until recently the locals spoke Norman-French.

This being so, you might be surprised by the fact that they are part of Britain at all. Above all, you might be somewhat amazed at French lack of enterprise in letting things stay that way. But then, when you consider that a couple of islands off Canada are part of Metropolitan France, maybe it's not so odd.

If the Channel Islands are very definitely not French, then

they're not quite English either (Jersey is eighty-five miles from England, fourteen from France). They have their own coins and bank notes, legal systems and courts of law.

Administratively, they are just as complicated. They are neither a part of the United Kingdom nor a colony and they are not represented in the United Kingdom Parliament. They owe allegiance to the British Crown.

The link goes back to those sea-wolves the Normans, who used the islands as one of their main maritime bases. For example, in the year 1031, Duke Robert, William the Conqueror's father, launched an invasion fleet against England. It was blown off-course and landed in Jersey. Being a good Viking ('Normans' being, of course, 'northmen', Vikings who had invaded and settled in that bit of France), he didn't let that put him off. He went and pillaged Brittany instead.

You could say that England is a colony of the Channel Islands; and I think the islanders sometimes do. Heraldry seems to bear out their seemingly extravagant assertion. Since the Conquest of 1066, the coat of arms of England and Wales remains the flag of the Normans, three lions. Two of those lions (leopards if you prefer. There seems some heraldic confusion about what type of beasts they actually are) represent the two parts of continental Normandy. The third is the Channel Islands; but when 'we' lost Normandy to the French, we held onto the Channel Islands (or did they hang on to us?).

At least that explains why the flag of Normandy is today only two lions. Why 'we' (the royal 'we' that is, for I'm talking of the crown here, not the state), still have three is a bit odd. Logically of course, 'we' should only have one, but our royal pretensions have yet to catch up with history. The Queen to this day has among her titles 'Duke of Normandy'.

By the time that I had racked my brain over these complications, we were nearly there. A fact that I was grateful for. These small boats are an education after the large ferries. On crossings such as the one we had just undergone, many parties that claim immunity to seasickness realise their mistake.

As we sailed into the shelter of Saint Aubin's Bay and edged towards the jetty at Saint Helier, I was feeling decidedly green myself. The beauties of the bay, with its ancient castle standing guard over the port, were a little lost on me. (The French have tried to invade once or twice, but they seem to have been half-hearted affairs, to say the least).

I staggered up the hill to the guesthouse in a mixed mood. I was delighted to be in Jersey and on dry land, but somewhat bemused by the unusual terms of my business 'jolly'. In keeping with the egalitarian principles of Monsieur Pierrot, all expenses, fare, hotel and so on, were paid by his staff.

It was at the guesthouse, after dropping my bags and while waiting for the show to start, that I met, and was offered a job by, Reg, a fellow exhibitor and the English 'boss' of another French immobilier. Well, he was the boss in so far as he ran the show and managed all the work. The legal boss was, as ever, the French holder of the *Carte Professionnelle.*

Reg's agency was in the north of Brittany. It was selling houses successfully to the English market. Now he wanted to expand into southern Normandy. He had, he said, heard of my dissatisfaction with Monsieur Pierrot. He was looking for someone who could speak both French and English, produce good property details and who could sell houses. He was sure that I was the man that he was looking for. As far as he was concerned, I had already passed my probationary period by selling houses for Monsieur Pierrot. Was I interested in working for him?

The proposal was quite simple; and not unfamiliar. Reg's agency wasn't working in Normandy, so I could draw my own boundaries, down into Brittany if I liked. I would be helped to find an office to work from. I would be sent customers and given help to find houses. And I would be paid for my petrol!

These were better conditions than I had already, and by now I was quite certain that Monsieur Pierrot had no intention of authorising my office. I had badgered that gentleman persistently, and even offered to pay the rent on the office myself (to be paid from sales), but he had merely told me to wait. I had had enough of waiting. I accepted Reg's offer.

However, I did not want help in finding property. I was quite capable of doing that for myself. In fact I enjoyed it. Also, I wanted my contract to state that I would be given my own office. I had been foolish enough to take the point on trust with Dick. Reg agreed with all that, although the contract might take a few weeks to draw up. Such was the legal system.

I agreed. To do so would mean throwing away several months work, but it would be worth it to get that office.

The exhibition opened. I was on Monsieur Pierrot's stall (with Dick, the great man himself being absent). Given that I was about to resign, it was with a certain lack of enthusiasm that I showed off my - by now excellent - book of properties.

Indeed, I considered throwing up the agency then and there and going for a grand stroll round the island. A twenty-five mile high speed march around the coast would have blown away a lot of devils. However, though I would draw no advantage from my work at the property show, and I was annoyed at Dick that the office he had promised me had not materialised, I was not about to let him down. So I carried on 'selling dreams' (Dick's term) until the final whistle. Then I went off for my walk.

With my passion for history, there was one aspect of Jersey that particularly interested me. That it is the chief of those islands which were the only part of Britain to fall to the Germans during the war.

A prize as prestigious as this was, thought Hitler, worth defending. Consequently he turned them into fortresses. To this day, the islands bristle with German fortifications. There is hardly a cove, beach or cliff-top which doesn't have its bunkers, observation towers or gun emplacements.

Hitler wasted his time. The Allies had no intention of stirring up this particular hornets' nest, preferring to bypass it and let it perish from lack of supplies. However, the nest still had a sting. After the July 1944 plot on his life, Hitler replaced all moderate commanders with hard line Nazis. In Jersey, this was Admiral Huffmeier. In one of the last actions of the war in Europe, the German garrison sailed out of Jersey, attacked Granville and destroyed harbour installations, killing several citizens. Militarily it was a completely pointless move.

Huffmeier finally surrendered a day after the rest of Germany, on the 9th May 1945, on the direct orders of Hitler's replacement, Admiral Donitz.

Alderney was the most notorious of the islands during the war, having three German labour camps, including the terrible SS Concentration camp, Lager Sylt, near the airport. With the British population evacuated en masse, it is thought that many hundreds of prisoners from eastern Europe (mainly Russians) died as slave workers, through malnutrition and sheer exhaustion. Even the birds are said to have fled the island.

The six thousand people who lived on Jersey and who were not born there (mostly from mainland Britain) were deported, some to their deaths. Those islanders who resisted and were caught were also deported, some to die in concentration camps. And the fortifications were created by slave labourers from a dozen conquered countries.

In Jersey, the grimmest reminder of those days is the vast underground military hospital. It was this that I visited. It was originally constructed as a bombproof artillery barracks and ammunition store, and designed to protect an entire army division from any assault from sea or air. It was converted into a casualty receiving station shortly before D-Day.

It is an amazing feat of engineering. The kilometre-long tunnels and galleries were fashioned out of the brittle shale with gunpowder and hand-tools. It was constructed mainly by Polish and Russian prisoners of war, slaves of the *Organization Todt*. These men toiled for twelve hours a day in an underground hell of dust, smoke and falling rock. The Todt organisation took its name from its founder, Fritz Todt. 'Tod' might have been more appropriate. That is the German word for death.

A visit to the museum brings home what occupation, even in its 'sanitised' version meant. The Channel Islands' wartime experiences were of evil. In the face of it was shown bravery, heroism, and active and passive resistance. There was also indifference, cowardice, and collaboration. All of these are unchangeable facets of humanity; and few of us can be sure which we would have shown if we had been there.

On the sea voyage back to Granville, I stood out on the deck and gazed over the stern rail at Jersey. Dick was out there too. The wind had not moderated over the last couple of days and he was looking very green round the gills.

"Curse the bloody Channel", he said, his eyes slits of pain

in his face.

I thought back to the Underground Hospital and the sorry story of the Channel Islands' war years.

"Funnily enough, Dick," I said, slapping him heartily on the back, "I was thinking the exact opposite."

Then I turned my eyes towards France.

SELLING FRENCH DREAMS

A Christmas visit. The Chaos battery.
Casualty. Christmas Day

On the twenty-third of December, we went on an outing.
We were going to see a very special lady. We had last met her,
well three of us had, several years earlier. David hadn't even
been born then. At that time we had been holidaying, not living,
in France and we had stayed in the lady's holiday cottage.
Today, God permitting, we would see her again.

One of the things that made the lady special, and the
reason why God's good grace was necessary, was the fact

that she was rather old. Even so, Madame had back then still been milking her herd, making her cider, pickling her cornichons (gherkins), growing her vegetables and cleaning and looking after the *Gite* that she had let out to us.

Madame was a very sweet old lady. Each morning we would go up to her farmhouse for milk and she would offer us the traditional wickedly-strong black coffee, liberally laced with calvados and with a sugar lump to dip in. I was the one most likely to succumb.

Madame dressed very simply and very traditionally. She wore wooden clogs, *sabots* (and incidentally the origin of the word 'sabotage' - literally to stick the boot in), a black skirt and a white blouse. She was small, with a very wrinkled, very friendly, face. She smiled a lot.

So we had decided to find Madame, if we could, and wish her a happy Christmas. Then we were to carry on to the coast, to visit a gun battery at Longues sur Mer, which I wanted to photograph to use as an illustration in my book. I am a romantic at heart.

The first challenge was to find the old lady's house. We knew that she lived in the north of the *Departement*, up towards Perriers, at a place called La Haye Pommeraye. The house was set pretty deeply in the bocage, miles from anywhere and on a complicated network of roads. Of course, on our holiday we had driven to and from the place every day for a week, so we both knew where it was. The trouble was, each one of us knew that it was in a different place.

In our household, contrary to most that I know, Ann tends to drive and I to read the map. She's a better driver than I am; indeed, spatially, most people are. I can not believe how drivers of container wagons can back them down narrow lanes by the side of shops. If it were up to me, I would either ram the wagon irretrievably in the lane or not manage to get into the opening at all. I tend to lose my cool on these occasions, so I would probably bolt from the scene of the crime. On one memorable occasion, I even backed one of our cars into the other one; thus presenting myself with the interesting conundrum of whether it would be worth-while claiming from myself, and what my defence would be.

Ann, while she has the spatial awareness that I lack, is not a practised map-reader. She has trouble with relating the map that she is holding to the countryside outside and deciding quickly where to go. Furthermore, under stress she suffers from a not-uncommon handicap. She can't always tell her left from her right.

As I was map-reading, I chose alternative 'A': where I knew the place to be, over alternative 'B': where Ann knew it to be. I might have known that it would be a mistake. Ann has a nasty habit of being right, and nowhere is this more obvious than in knowing where things are. I suppose being constantly barraged with questions such as:

"Have you seen my socks?"

"Have you seen my coat?"

"Have you seen that book I was reading?"

May have helped develop the faculty. Whatever the reason, it is there.

By the time I had admitted my mistake and we had gone for alternative 'B', it was getting towards noon. It was a typical Norman winter's day; fog-bound from morning until night. I suppose it is the fact that we were living on a peninsula; or perhaps it was due to the millions upon millions of trees breathing quietly to themselves, but it was usually foggy. In summer, the sun would burn it off. In winter it just hung around all day; as it did today.

Isolated hamlets loomed out of the dripping half-light and, in silence, disappeared again. Cows glowered over farm gates. It wouldn't have been surprising if a horse-drawn hearse had loomed up, the coachman thrashing his horses wildly and the sharp features of Peter Cushing glowered down at us from a grimy half-light.

Eventually, we found the place. The isolated holiday cottage that we had stayed at was empty at this time of the year.

The place gave me the creeps. I had had an odd experience there, which I had not shared with Ann at the time, but which heightened my sense of gloom.

It was a two bedroom cottage; Alice's cot had been in one bedroom and Ann and I in the other. Alice was a light sleeper as a baby and would wake up in a paddy. As I tolerate lack of sleep better than Ann, I was usually the one who would get up to carry her (Alice that is!) around until she dropped-off (up and down the stairs was her favourite. Good healthy exercise, but not wholly welcome at three in the morning).

That night, Alice was slightly feverish, so even likelier than usual to wake up. As well as the cot, Alice's room also contained a double bed, so I decided to sleep there. Consequently, Ann 'went on up', while I sat by the log fire with my calvados and cigar and read a bit more of my book. Finally, I went my way up the uncarpeted stairs and across the wooden floor of the infant's room - the floor creaking angrily despite my efforts to be as light as a mouse.

The double bed was between the door and Alice's cot. I undressed and climbed in. I was just drifting through that delicious half-sleep when, sometimes, you have enough consciousness to manipulate your dreams a little, when I heard steps coming up the stairs. Being only partly 'there', I put

74

it down to Ann coming up to bed.

The steps sounded nearer now. Coming into the room. They came across the floor and stopped beside the bed. Beside me. Suddenly, as realisation came, I woke up. I was scared. Terrified. Struck motionless with fear. It took a lot of effort and probably a good ten minutes before I could summon up will and courage enough to reach for my cigarette lighter. There was, of course, nothing there.

For the remaining few days of our holiday, I slept alone in Alice's room. I told Ann that I had a cold and would only keep her awake. I didn't get much sleep; but there was no re-occurrence of the event. I told Ann about it on the ferry back to England.

I suppose that coming from York, which has an atmosphere all of its own - and where in the old churches and manors I have had one or two odd experiences - I am perhaps more susceptible than most to atmosphere. Maybe I owe it to my grandmother who was 'fey'. At any rate, it gave me a shiver to see the cottage loom out of the mist.

The farmstead lay perhaps a quarter of a mile up the lane behind the cottage. At the end of the lane was a gate, which I got out to open. As I did so, I was surprised to see three men standing by the side of the small farmhouse. They were dressed in the regulation 'blues' (denim overalls) of the French countryside. As I walked up to them, the eldest of them, a beetle-browed, frowning man of late middle age, detached himself slightly from the other two.

"What do you want?" The question was half suspicious, half hostile.

In truth, none of them seemed happy to see me. Was our errand a waste of time? Had Madame passed over and left the smallholding to this surly trio? I explained my mission. I was English (that was evident!). My family and I, or at least three of us, had stayed in Madame's holiday cottage a few years back. We had liked her very much and had come to wish her the season's compliments.

After a moment's incomprehension, the atmosphere and the faces cleared. Was Madame still with us? *Bien sur*! She was indoors! Come in, come in!

We trooped inside. The place was exactly as we remembered it; except that whereas before we had been confined to the small kitchen, now we were shown into the main room. It was a typical Norman room. Small windows, a great ticking subtly-hipped Grandfather clock, the floor of beaten clay. A dark place with beautiful, spare, old wooden furniture and, as ever, spoiled by a huge, incongruous and dominating television. In the great granite hearth was the fire, piled up with logs.

There were two other people in the room: Madame herself, and her great grand-daughter, a girl in her early twenties. Madame's eyes were a little more rheumy maybe, but she was still the sweet, smiling old lady whom we remembered. The men were her son and his two sons. Then came the shock. Madame was one hundred years old!

Ann presented our little gift: a tin of English chocolates, not much, but much prized by the French, who make no such thing themselves. Everyone was introduced.

The older man coughed apologetically. "You must forgive our reception, Monsieur. You are so tall. Looming out of the mist like that, we thought that you were an official." (I don't know why being tall makes people think like that, but it undoubtedly does).

Now that the ice was broken, what more natural in Normandy

than to celebrate with the pressings of the apple? We were greeted as long-lost friends. In the dark and dragging winter days, there is not much that can be done on the farm; and not much in the way of distraction either. Any excuse for a knees-up is welcome. So we set-to to cement the good feelings between the English and the Normans with house calvados.

Calvados is distilled cider, and the spirit of choice in Normandy. Its production is closely controlled by the state, which is gradually removing from the unlicensed individual the right to make it at all. It does this by only allowing farmers who have been farming since before 1958 to make the stuff; and then only ten litres per annum. However, the country people don't always see things in this light; and it is certain that a lot more of it is made than is declared, and quite possibly that was what the men thought I had come about. If so, they made up for their error by plying me with it in earnest.

While the young woman played with Alice and David, we menfolk got stuck into the booze and proceeded to put the world to rights. Ann's subtle indications that I was overdoing it were ignored. I was enjoying this! And besides, I wasn't driving.

Finally, and bearing in mind that we still had to visit the coast, it was time to leave. As a matter of fact, Ann had a bit of trouble winkling me out. The kindly Norman family had invited us to stay for lunch and I was all for accepting. What harm could a few more drinks do? Then a sing-song perhaps. That plan might have been slightly marred by the fact that the only song that I know all the verses to is 'Ilkley Moor Baht 'At', which I sometimes used to serenade Ann with when we were courting, on the way back to her flat in the Royal Crescent in Bath, after an evening down town. (Yes, good citizens of Aqua Sulis, that was me, and I'm sorry).

I was half-cut. No, I was inebriated. No, I was under the influence. No, I was drunk. Worse, I was three sheets to the wind, one over the eight, high as a kite, legless, intoxicated, befuddled, blotto, blasted, pickled, pie-eyed, plastered, steaming, sloshed, smashed, sozzled. And that's just putting it politely. With many protestations of eternal friendship, the children and their mother steered me back to the car.

We stopped off at a small town on the way to the coast to get something to eat. It was, as I've said, a very grey day. The warm light of the restaurant on the edge of the *Place* spilled over onto the pavement and tempted us in. The restaurant was bustling; everyone seemed to be relaxed and happy that Christmas was so close.

We selected our starters from the fish and cold meats, settled down with the main course (a casserole with chestnuts) and worked our way through to the *Buche de Noel* - the Christmas log. By now I was drinking water furiously to try to sober up a little. "Another carafe Monsieur? Why certainly." My eyes were beginning to close and my head felt as if a sleepy cat had taken up lodging.

"David's not eating." Ann sounded worried. Indeed for a boy who, judging by the fact that he tries to eat twice his own weight every twenty-four hours, was presumably a vole in a previous existence, this was remarkable. But I had my own problems.

I'm afraid that my map reading to the coast may not have been of the highest standard. The children seemed a little puzzled too.

"Why's daddy talking funny?"

"I'm not talking funny, I'm perfectly sober. I could drive this car as well as your mother." This, as it was to transpire, was a dangerous delusion.

Finally, we arrived at the Chaos Battery (I don't think that it was specially named for out visit, but the name was to prove pretty appropriate nevertheless) at Longues sur Mer.

This battery of four guns, along with an observation post, was constructed by the Germans during the Second World War as part of the Atlantic Wall, their coastal defences against the threatened Allied invasion. It was overwhelmed on D. Day. The concrete blockhouses are the best preserved anywhere on the coast and the most evocative. They are pockmarked by shells.

The first of the four guns is completely destroyed and unrecognisable, but the other three are just as they were after the duel. You can put your fists through the holes made by the shells that finished them off.

One wonders at the bravery of those gunners, shooting at the hundreds of approaching ships while one after another of them was silenced, and at the skill of the gunners out at sea who managed from a range of several miles to lob shells right onto the guns.

The defenders were expendable. Some weeks before the landings, Rommel (in charge of the fortifications) had complained to Hitler about the lack of mobility of his troops. "Their role is to stay in their fortifications and die behind their guns," the Fuehrer had said, "so they don't need to be mobile."

We toured the installation together, the children happily playing hide and seek, myself doing a passable impersonation of a mole just woken from hibernation (if moles do hibernate): myopic, bad tempered and misanthropic. Ann was mostly silent. I took my photographs and we headed back towards the car.

The guns at Longues sur Mer are not sited directly at the top of the cliffs but at the top of the slope above them. That slope from the guns to the cliff top is greatly eroded by the hundreds of rabbits who make their warrens there. Being chalk, it is also slippery, even more so than usual on this dank and foggy day.

It may have been the slipperiness, perhaps it was a rabbit hole, but for one reason or the other, Ann fell over beside me. Lost in my own calva-clouded world, I at first didn't properly understand what had happened. Then David, more alert than I, pulled on my arm.

"Help mummy!" I did as I was told. Ann was in pain and could not support her weight. I hauled her to her feet and put her arm round my shoulder. With my non-too steady assistance on one side and the childrens' valiant efforts on the other, we got her up the slope and into the car park.

"I think I've broken it." She was in real pain.

"You certainly choose your moments don't you!"

"Do you think I did it on purpose!" Her rebuke was in anger and pain; said through tears. I almost felt contrite.

"Can you walk now?"

"Daddy, didn't you hear what mummy said? She thinks she's broken it."

Ours was the only car in the car park. There were no phones.

"Then I'll have to take you to hospital." Had Ann been in less pain, she would, I have no doubt, have dissuaded me. As it was, I looked at the map, saw that the nearest hospital was in Bayeux and set out.

It was dark now and a light rain was falling. Have I mentioned that I was over the limit? I've never driven a car when drunk before (or since). I suppose there are two types of drunken driver, the one who drives exaggeratedly slowly and the one who drives without a care in the world. I was of the slow school and at first all went well. So near to Christmas, there was not much traffic in the Norman countryside.

It was after I got on the main road that I began to have terrible doubts. Bayeux is not a huge town, but it's big enough, and I had no idea where the hospital was.

Fate seemed to be on my side when I saw a couple of hitch hikers (a boy and girl). I stopped and asked them where they were going. Bayeux. They must have been a little surprised to be given a lift by an English family with two little kids, who had to move their booster seats so that they could get in; and it was quite a squeeze with their rucksacks.

When I explained our predicament, they set about guiding me through the streets; and I'm very glad they did, what with the chains of Christmas lights festooned everywhere and the tipsy pedestrians attempting suicide beneath my wheels. Actually, I'm not sure that a French pedestrian has much choice but to duck and dive and take his chances. It's always a matter of conjecture what the pedestrian crossings are for in France. There are hundreds of them in towns, but as car drivers simply ignore them, they seem to be a kind of outdoor relief for itinerant line-painters.

By this time, the gravity of the situation was beginning to percolate through the alcohol in my skull. When I was a kid at school, I ran into another child and fell over. And couldn't move. My brother Peter, in that charming way of siblings, assumed that I was faking and tried to pull me up. Luckily a teacher dragged him off.

The ambulance arrived and I was carted off to hospital where I was found to have broken my leg. The simplest of mishaps and three months in plaster. What if Ann's leg was broken? Should I have moved her? Had I just made things worse? How could I look after the kids and her and work at the same time?

And it was a tipsy time of year. What Byzantine complexities was the visit to the hospital going to land us in? Would Casualty be filled with psychopathic motorcyclists, or chain-sawn farmers?

How would we go about reclaiming the costs of this visit? The French system is absurdly complex at the best of time, with forms, stickers (*vignettes*), copies, signatures, counter signatures and insurance companies. I was certain the French medical system would be up to the emergency - but would we spend the rest of our lives tied hand and foot in red tape?

We finally reached the hospital. The two hitch-hikers melted quickly and gratefully into the shadows and we were left to our own devices.

I am very happy to say that Casualty was a disappointing place in terms of dramatic possibilities. With a couple of young children in tow (and David was beginning to look a little green), in a foreign land and in an alcoholic haze, I wouldn't have liked to deal with a sub-Hitchcock plot.

The place was deserted. Very quickly, Ann was put onto a trolley and wheeled off to be x-rayed. Leaving the long-suffering and confused children to be looked after by a pair of very charming nurses (I was a bit worried about David), I followed her.

The x-ray was taken and developed. Ann had merely strained muscles in her calf. A plaster-impregnated bandage was wound tight around it. It could come off in a week. There would be no need to come back unless there were complications, which looked unlikely. A few days rest in bed was what was needed. She was lent a pair of crutches. These could be returned to our local doctor. As far as all the forms and bureaucracy went, the medics did what any sensible French person in a position of authority does. Ignored them.

Using a combination of her new crutches and what help I could give, Ann hobbled across the courtyard of the hospital and to the car. With her seat back as far as it would go and her foot poked out rigidly into the footwell, I drove us slowly home. I don't suppose my driving helped matters for David, but bless his heart he waited until we got home and he was out of the car before he was sick.

Christmas Eve dawned. Both David and I were struck down by a mystery illness. Perhaps mine was a little less mysterious than his. Ann was, of course, laid up. Alice, just turned eight, was mother. We had not done the Christmas shop, so when a friend of ours, Louise, rang for a chat, she was unfortunate enough to be on the receiving end of a tale of woe. She rose to the occasion and did the shopping for us.

By evening, David was much better, Ann was sitting up, Alice was reaping well-deserved praise, Flavie was fed-up through lack of a walk and I had made the customary vow to swear off alcohol for the rest of my life.

At least we managed to wrap up the presents. Tomorrow would be a better day.

Of course, for the parents of small children, Christmas Day rarely starts as 'a better day'. The little horrors seem to think that an appropriate time for *reveillé* is around four o'clock in the morning. But eventually, when the bed had all but disappeared under wrapping paper (in which Flavie was happily playing) and presents, we ungummed our eyes and looked out on the world.

We were to cook Christmas Dinner on and in the gas cooker. Gas is really the only feasible way of cooking in the French countryside

I don't really like to compare French and English institutions as a rule. It gets a bit like a childish match:

"You should call your chocolate 'solidified vegetable fats'"

"Think so do you? Well your 'Golden-Delicious' apple should be called 'green blotting-paper'. Oh, and while I think about it, Johnny Halliday's rubbish!"

"Yeah? Yeah? Well your major contribution to post-war Europe has been mad cow disease'"

"Well what about Général de Gaulle?"

"You burnt Joan of Arc."

So I shall not dwell on the contrariness, inefficiency and wayward pricing structure of the French electricity supply. I will simply say that no-one in their right mind would try cooking with electricity.

Some hybrid stoves, half electric, half gas, can be had; but they still use that dangerous component, electricity, so we had never been tempted to buy one of those. Ours was the gas-bottle variety.

Under Ann's direction, I soon had the vegetables prepared, the batter done, the chicken de-gibleted and be-baconed and the rest of the preparations done.

Soon the Yorkshire puddings were rising, the vegetable water beginning to boil, the onions for the gravy chopped up and the chicken starting to brown. I went into the living room to gently see whether I was up to a pre-lunch whisky. I looked with satisfaction at the logs blazing merrily in the grate. A dog, two cats and two children were on the settee. *Chitty Chitty Bang Bang* (a Christmas present) was on the video, and the kids were firing sucker darts at the baddies. Ah Christmas at last! Now, I just had David's new lego castle to finish and I would be able to relax.

"Alan." Ann was calling from the kitchen. "Darling, the gas has failed. Can you put the spare on?"

The voice was too sweetly reasonable. She knew it was Gotterdammerung just as well as I did. I had meant to replace the spare for a week and would doubtless have done so on the previous day if my major pre-occupation had not been simply surviving.

What made it even worse, if that was possible, was that Ann had reminded me two or three times about it in the last week. If there is anything with more potential savagery than a man without an excuse, it is, perhaps, the woman who has found him out.

She took the trouble to hobble outside, with stick and crutch, as I dumped the empty gas bottle in the boot of the car. "And don't come back without it!" She yelled at me.

The children stood accusing and silent, one on each side of their mother. It was like a cross between *Treasure Island* and *The Midwich Cuckoos*.

Flavie jumped in beside me as I got into the car. I think she must have been feeling sorry for me. I certainly was.

Our house lies between Percy and the cross-roads hamlet of Villebaudon. Percy being by far the largest of these settlements, I naturally tried the town first. I had no luck. Christmas Day? Where was going to be open on Christmas Day? The answer was simple. Nowhere.

It was only as an act of desperation that I drove up to Villebaudon, the empty gas bottle rolling in the boot like the knell of doom as I climbed the long hill.

"And don't come" (bump) "back without it!" (bump).

The hamlet has but one shop, where I was wont to buy my beer and the bottled gas. As ever, the gas was there but chained up. The main road was deserted, the shop was closed for Christmas.

Just then, Flavie leaped from the car and hurled herself barking at the shop window, where one of her old adversaries was enjoying the weak winter sunshine. Flavie is a much braver and more aggressive dog if there is a chain, gate, window or door between her and the object of her anger.

That was it! "Shut up!" I screamed at the cur, venting my frustration on her.

A window shot open above the shop and the face of the owner peered out. "*Joyeux Noel, Monsieur Bee-geen.*"

"And a happy Christmas to you too."

"You have not stocked up with enough beer?"

I winced. I was still not fully recovered. "I believe that I have stocked up with enough beer to last me for the rest of my life. Unfortunately I do not expect that that life is going to last much longer."

"But that is very serious. Let me come down to you."

Soon, the bolt was drawn back and I was explaining my predicament. Instead of telling me to go to hell for disturbing his Christmas, I was invited in for a drink.

"Oh, go on then, a quick one. Just a little one though. But it is Christmas."

My gas cylinder was exchanged.

I made sure that Flavie got the giblets.

French lessons. By British firesides.
Obsession. White out.

My mother's letter arrived shortly after Christmas. I propped it up against the *Bonne Maman* jar and read it as I ate my breakfast baguette. The letter wished us a happy and prosperous new year and gave the usual gratuitous advice that comes from mothers; keep the kids wrapped up warm, don't forget to wash behind your ears, try for matching shoes and socks where possible. It ended up by saying '...if the property market doesn't really pick up until April, it looks as if you're in for a lazy couple of months.'

On the face of it, my mother's remark appeared accurate. The winter is indeed a dead time for selling property. At any rate it is as far as selling French property to the British goes. Property still comes in of course. If the customers did but know it, the best time to buy is sometime between January and April, before the season kicks in. By then there is a backlog of houses on the books built up from the previous autumn onwards, some of which the owners are desperate to sell. Also, you tend to get a more sober view of a house when it is in its winter colours.

However, few people want to tackle the Channel in winter, with short cold days for viewing and who can blame them?

Even if I had not much to do on the housing front, I had one or two 'background tasks' to keep me out of mischief.

First, given that I had my exams in May, it was essential that I keep my French up to scratch. To do that, I needed both to write and speak the language and, most vital of all, to have my mistakes corrected. I had got into the habit of starting any conversation in French with the words: "Please excuse my French and I would be grateful if you could tell me when I make a mistake." By and large I was wasting my time. People are too nice to correct such errors. They just make allowances for them. They may even find them charming or endearing, as I do myself when listening to a French person speaking English.

That's all very considerate and useful in everyday speech, but less than useless when you're preparing for an exam, as it simply reinforces mistakes and bad habits. This was the down-side of not learning in a classroom with a teacher. So I had to find my own teachers. Consequently I met up with several French friends for fifty-fifty French and English conversation.

There was my good friend Doctor Marais and his wife in their large old, comfortable house. Here I was privileged not only to be taught history, as I have related elsewhere, but philosophy and grammar. I shall never forget being told-off by Madame Marais for being sloppy in my pronunciation of 'Oui', a bad habit I had slipped into from talking to the kids and their friends.

"On dit oui pas ouaii Monsieur!" I have rarely pronounced it *ouaii* (yeah) since!

Then there was Nelly, the vet's wife. Nelly was learning English just as I was learning French, and to the same level, only hers was a much more structured course, from the University of Caen. We would often meet up. One half of the *rencontre* would be devoted to English, the other to French. She would correct my grammatical gaffes and written work. I would give her what advice I could about what Donne or Shakespeare had *really* been driving at.

Nelly and her husband, Pascal, had a dog, a great white Husky which Nelly would take for unusual walks in the quiet lanes in her part of the Commune. She would drive the car while her daughter held the dog's lead out of the window and the dog trotted alongside. If she'd had a few more hounds like that, she could have dispensed with the car altogether.

Then there was Natalie, a Breton teacher of English at the kids' school. I think she was a bit lonely. She spoke excellent English so I wasn't much help to her, but she certainly helped me.

So I was up to four or five 'lessons' a week. In 'the French bit' of the lessons, we would go through and correct the two page essays that I churned out each and every day on some aspect of French life.

So much for preparing for my exams.

I was also preparing a course for British people who were considering emigrating to France. The idea for the course had come from a discussion that I had had with Dick. He had been bemoaning the fact that he could not sell the house that he had bought when he first moved to Normandy. He had made a big mistake buying in such an isolated position, and he'd paid far too much for the property. Now, although he was asking considerably less than he'd paid for the place, he could not get rid of it. That was only one of the problems that he had experienced.

"It wouldn't be so bad if it was just me," he told me, "but you see the same mistakes being made time and time again. The place is littered with Brits with problems. Broken marriages, bankruptcies, health, you name it. Half of the people who come over here sell up and move back to Britain within two years - or try to. I wish someone would tell them."

Terrible though it was, what Dick said was true. The same problems occurred time and again; and claimed a massive number of casualties. In my own small way, I had tried to address some of those problems in the leaflets that I had produced; but what I was doing was very minor. What was needed was a course which pointed out the pitfalls inherent in moving to France; and how they could be avoided. If I could put together and stage such a course, it would not only be profitable to me, it could - no, it would - save many of those who attended it from misery and loss.

To find out what those pitfalls were, I was carrying out a survey of the experiences and opinions of every British person whom I knew who already lived in France. I thought I already knew some of the answers, but I wanted to hear it 'from the horse's mouth'. Who, after all, knew more about living as expatriates than those who were already doing so?

To do this, I prepared a questionnaire. This covered two sides of an A4 sheet of paper and consisted of more than fifty questions. It asked about experiences in buying property, making a living, day to day life, health, education and socialising; what had the respondents got right? What had they got wrong? What had been the consequences? If they were to go through the move again, what would they do differently? 'What three things should those who are moving to France take into account?'

Initially I gave several copies of the questionnaire to a couple of English friends. I asked them if they would fill out the forms themselves, and also pass on copies to any other British expatriates who they knew, with the request that they ring me if they were happy for me to visit them to go through the form. I've interviewed quite a lot of people in my time, and I knew from work that I had done in the past that generally people will only complete surveys if you're sitting down with them.

I got a very good response. Consequently, in the first three months of the year, I needed to visit around thirty houses. Normally, we would sit by the fire while my respondents filled in the form. The process usually took a couple of hours.

I had been nervous about some of the questions; for example about health and stress. However, when they knew what the survey was for, and when I had assured them of the confidentiality of their answers, people talked freely. In my experience, folk will talk quite openly about their lives, and even their problems, if they know that it is in a good cause.

I was very grateful to my British friends for granting me their time and their expertise. If I could, I would try to reciprocate by doing some small favour for them. Translating a form into English perhaps, or phoning up a French tradesman or local government department. I didn't mind. It was all grist to the mill.

(Apart from the forty 'hands on' interviews that I did, I was also to speak to a further sixty people on the phone in the weeks that followed; but these I asked only one question: their advice to others who intended making the same move as they had done.)

Then I had to prepare the course itself. As well as the input from the survey, I had to also incorporate technical sections about the law and building regulations. These I developed with the help of friends who are expert in those fields, and who were to help me put on the course.

I ended up with over a hundred pages of notes, covering lots of different subjects. I estimated that the course would take two days. Prepare, test, revise. Test, revise, test. I wanted them to be perfect.

In those dark winter months, I was also to fall prey to an obsession. I'm a bit prone to obsessive behaviour. When I was a kid, I would play patience endlessly rather than doing my homework. Later in life it was 'Digger' on the computer. If I have a crossword, I can't give up until it's solved. Sometimes my obsessive character has stood me in good stead; for instance when I've been curing computer software 'bugs'. Sometimes it's a damned pain to myself and all around me. This time, the obsession centred on the book that I was writing, which I had provisionally called *A Normandy Tapestry* (I know, I know).

I had been working on that for months, at weekends, in the evenings and in the early mornings. It had been difficult enough to write, not least when, in the middle of chapter twelve, revision seven, my computer broke down. Had I backed it up? I am a computer professional of twenty-five years standing. Of course not.

I parcelled the thing up and sent it back to England, to my sister Joan, a computer engineer. She repaired it and sent it back. Two weeks' delay. I've backed the machine up since then (the same thing happened while I was writing this book. A lightning storm struck the phone lines, travelled up into both computers in the house, cooking both. Act of God or the other guy?)

Lord or Lucifer notwithstanding, I finally got the work to the point where I could submit it for publication. I sent copies out to many an English publisher. They were returned for a variety of reasons.

Some were of the opinion that too many books were already being published. Others advised that they could not publish as many as they would have liked. Some told me that, yes I could write and they liked my work, but it would be a lot easier to sell my book if I was to first distinguish myself in another profession; as a television celebrity, or a sports or rock star maybe. Fame. That's what's needed to sell books on 'foreign parts'.

I tried. I kicked a ball around a bit, bowled at some stumps that I drew on the barn door. I even tried singing. I think that René's cows were quietly impressed, but no talent spotter leaped out of the bushes. Nor did the experience much increase my fund of tales. And it didn't improve my ability to write at all.

Other than advising me to become famous, the publishing industry, although unfailingly polite, wasn't much use to me. Did I need them though? I believed that my book had an audience in the millions who visit the shops on the ferries between England and France and who are looking for 'a good read' during a week or two without television. They, I thought, would be more interested in the subject than in the name on the spine.

By this time I was like a duck swallowing a worm, or Macbeth wading across his stream. There was no way I would (or maybe even could) turn back. So, on the basis of 'if you can't join them, beat them', I decided to go it alone and publish the thing myself. Hadn't I done most of the hard work already in writing it? Well, yes. But putting my words between covers, and getting the resultant book onto shelves, was to give me plenty to keep me occupied during my 'lazy couple of months'.

I took it a step at a time.

What I had written so far was far from good enough. In writing, as in anything else we do, the easiest thing in the world is to ignore our own faults. I needed outsiders to look at my work, correct grammatical blunders and point out where I was going wrong. So I asked a few friends to read it, and was able to greatly improve the book as a result.

Then there were the technical bits. How do you lay out pages? What typeface do you use? What about 'leading' (the space between lines. The term comes from the time when typesetters used lead for the job). What about tracking (the space between the letters). What about page layout and headings and footings? A few years ago, those mysteries were all-but unfathomable to the layman; but nowadays they can be solved with a little application and a software package.

Of course a nice cover was vital. Again I needed help. After a good deal of searching, I had found an artist who was excellent at drawing buildings (and it was on this basis that I had selected him). Unfortunately he was not too hot on people.

A LAZY COUPLE OF MONTHS

Luckily I had shown the book to an acquaintance, Roger, (now a friend) who is a graphic artist. He was very complimentary and recommended Tony Beesley, who lives in France. This time there was no mistake. Tony was superb. I gave him pictures of the house, the kids, René and Thérèse and told him what I wanted. He painted a wonderful cover. I approved the work and he took it away to make a slight adjustment. Over the weekend Tony tidied up his workroom and threw out the rubbish. Including my cover. Artists!

He repainted it in forty-eight hours, but it wasn't the same. Something about the deepness of the purple in the trees in the background was wrong. Would anyone notice it? Do I notice it several reprints later? No and no. But I was obsessed.

Obsession really took hold when I realised that there are a hundred links in the chain of success; and that every one of them must be sound. In those circumstances, obsession isn't a fault. It's essential. That's my excuse anyway.

Questions kept coming up. Where was I to get the bar code on the back of the book and the international catalogue number (ISBN)? How do you put text onto a cover? How much could I charge for the book? The standard for book prices seems to be so many pounds, 99p. I thought '99p' was just silly, but in the end I didn't have the guts to go against received book-selling wisdom. I may be a Yorkshireman, but I'm not Guy Fawkes.

How big should the book be? How many pages should it have? What, for legal purposes, did I need to put on the first couple of pages? Some kind of notification about copyright, piracy and so on?

What should I call it? That was vitally important. The wrong decision here can kill a book stone dead. Looking round my bookshelves, I sometimes ask myself who else but I would ever have purchased:

'Blind white fish in Persia' (about a caving expedition)
'40,000 against the Arctic' (a heroic history of Soviet
bravery in exploiting the polar regions. Sounds bad
odds for the Arctic to me)
'Congenital goitres in Dutch goats'
'Radiation cookery'
'Take my wife' by Gay Talese

(If you find such titles as amusing as I do, then the next time that you are in London, I advise you to stand at the gates of the British Museum, looking outwards, go across the road and walk a few yards to the right. You will find a bookshop there whose window is full of second-hand books, selected for their ridiculous titles. I can guarantee you a hoot.)

No, the title must be good, and it should also reflect the book. In the end, I stuck with *A Normandy Tapestry*, with the subtitle 'A portrait of rural France.' It didn't seem to me to be very strong, but it did reflect the contents, a weave of family, selling houses, rural life and the story of Normandy itself.

The harder I worked, and the deeper I got into the book, the less sociable I became. All this time, I was working in the spare bedroom with the shutters closed to keep in the heat. A dark, cold, miserably intellectual existence.

I have always preferred jobs with a physical side. In computing, I'm quite happy to lug printers and screens about as well as plan communications networks or specify systems. This can be a double-edged sword. The computer industry is a heavy user of labels; not least on its staff. If you are seen carrying kit about, you will be labelled 'labourer'. It's a risk I've always taken. Exercise is essential to my well-being. In this case, also to keep me warm!

In between bouts of writing, phoning, planning and so on, I

would take myself out to the barn and saw wood. The hardwood that I had moved off the septic tank for Monsieur Fouchard. Eventually I would have a pile of logs for the fire, then it would be back to work.

I needed to commission a number of drawings for the book. Luckily, Erica, a friend of Ann's, is an artist and could do it. So I wrote to her and explained what I needed. She did an excellent job.

Of course, the reviews on the back of a book help to sell it. Professional publishers have whole departments dealing with publicity, and close links with newspapers and magazines. How was I to get my book reviewed? And how was I to do so before it was printed? I didn't bother with the national newspapers. I simply didn't have the time. Next time maybe. But I sent draft copies to those magazines with an interest in France. I was very pleased with the reviews.

Then there was the matter of printing. I asked for a number of quotes from printers, which varied alarmingly. Finally, I went to visit three. From them, it became obvious that in order to get the best economies of scale, I would need to print three thousand copies. I placed the order. The die was cast.

Now the jitters started in earnest. Three thousand books! I had to sell three thousand books! What if the publishing world had been right and there was no market for them? (Of course, in reality, there is no such thing as a monolithic 'publishing world', just a collection of often-competing people; but when you're alone - and I think that this is an affliction that mostly affects men - you tend to see indifference as part of a co-ordinated plan to 'do you down'). Three thousand books! I had to sell three thousand books!

By now I was a one-track creature, more of an automaton

than a man. Every link must be sound! No link must fail! I carried with me the whole time the over-riding urge: Must get this right! Obsession, obsession, obsession! Writing (and to a lesser extent publishing) the book was far, far harder than anything that I had ever done in computing, although that background certainly helped - for I was used to balancing a hundred considerations at once; and planning a sequence in which to do them.

The weeks raced by. The books arrived, Sixty nine boxes, each containing forty four books. Three thousand and thirty six books. Three for the British Library (no, please, my pleasure!), one for Ann, one for Alice and one for David. A few for my helpers. Stacks of boxes filling the whole of the utility room. The sink was inaccessible, the shelves were hidden, the washing machine difficult to get to. Hmm. Perhaps it was time to tackle Sales and Marketing.

I had had the book accepted by the ferries before I went ahead and printed it. That was the one link in my chain that was quite out of my control. For that chain to work, someone along the line had to look at the book and believe in it. As in all such matters, the first such act of faith is the most significant. After that, others tend to follow. The gentlemen's name, in this case, was Beat Wehren, a Purser (whatever that might involve) of one of the boats. Thank you Mr Wehren. You are in the Biggins' Hall of Fame.

As well as the ferries, however, I fancied that I would need other outlets too. So I decided to approach book shops near the south coast of England. But how was I going to get them to stock my self-published work? Wouldn't the perception be that I would have produced a ring-binder full of poorly typed pages, covered with crossings-out and tea stains, with the odd crisp packet pressed in here and there? I would have to speak to them to explain the book. I would try and get them to stock it there and then, but if necessary I would offer to send them a copy for review.

The prospect terrified me but, scared or not, it was (yet another) vital link. So I prepared a sales speech. Sell, sell, sell! What the book was about, what discount I offered, how I would invoice them. What my trading terms were (sale or return).

Getting through on the phone was the first hurdle. Often enough the buyer was serving a customer, having a break, on holiday. Finally, the conversation. A few rejections, but usually:

"Yes, we'll take six."

"We'll try two."

"Put us down for four."

"Send me a copy. If I like it, I'll place an order."

"Darling, can you pick up the kids from school today?"

Work, work, work. If the car firm (Avis, I think) can make an advertising campaign about having to try harder because they're only number two, they should try being number two thousand and two! Obsession, obsession, obsession. Ann knew that the single-mindedness, however essential it might be to realise my aim, was also corrosive. That the mountain of work was filling the whole of my vision, blocking out all else. And that was not healthy for me, her, the kids. So she would pull me back, get me to become part of the family again.

I would drive down the hill to Percy, park outside the school and wander for a couple of minutes in front of the gates, my mind full of lists and questions and jobs and dove-tailing commitments, my smile a mere rictus. Then the kids would come out and I would start to wind down.

"I won three marbles today. Look, the *terres*. They're the

ones I like best."

"Monsieur Brochard said my essay was the best in class. He's pinned it on the wall."

"Can we drive the car on super-bounce today?"

"They say that it's going to snow next week."

"Can I invite Caroline over?" (Caroline is René's grand daughter, and the then love of David's life).

...........a scatter-shot approach to getting my books into shops was only part of the answer. I would be better targeting outlets with lots of customers who might be interested in the work. Shops that specialised in things to do with France. Shops actually in France, with lots of British visitors but not much in English. I would have to design promotional material. Posters.

Damn! Why was that idiot turning left with so little warning?

.........leaflets, that was a thought! Leaflets with useful information on one side; how to phone the U.K. from France, a recipe for stuffed oysters, the rules about driving in bad weather. On the other side, an advert for the book. Would an insert in specialist magazines work? When? What about selling in hotels, museums, gift shops?

"Daddy, what's for tea?"

"Daddy, you nearly missed the turning."

Obsession, obsession, obsession!

"I'm just going upstairs to get on with it."

"Could you chop an onion for me first? And can you go through that French homework with David."

Then, back upstairs to get on with it. I'd really bitten off more than I could chew in my 'lazy couple of months'. Each day I had to write an essay for my exams. Then there were all the English/French study sessions that I was doing. I was still going out to do surveys; and I had more work to do on my course.

There were plenty more bookshops to be contacted: I had a list of half a dozen telephone calls to make each day (at that rate, I realise that I'll never make a tele-sales person: but to be honest it was all I had the courage for). And I had to design a mailshot for the book. I only hoped that some of this would bear fruit one day.

At last, at maybe ten at night, downstairs to unwind. Sitting in an armchair, smoking a cigar (is there an addiction stronger than nicotine? I gave up cigarettes twenty years ago, but can still not shake off my evening cigar). A drink of beer.

Those months were fuelled by beer and baccy, the only way I could unwind. After an hour of this, I would stumble off to bed, brain running-on like the engine of a badly-timed car. Fist clenched. Punching the air in weariness as I climbed the stairs. "I will succeed!" Obsessed, obsessed, obsessed. A damned pain to live with.

One evening I came down to see a note on the table. It was just a dog-eared bit of paper torn from a note book. But what it said was quite terrifying:

> "You get drunk.
> You spend all your money on yourself
> That's enough"

I went cold. The criticism was a bit strong. Yes, I got drunk, but I wasn't aware of spending all my money on myself, except on beer and tobacco of course, and in the grand scheme of household expenses that was minimal. It wasn't 'my' money anyway. And why had she underlined that particular point? Still, there it was. She had written the note for me to see. 'That's enough'. The message was clear. What was she going to do? Leave me? Surely she couldn't be thinking of that. Not Ann. Not the centre. But there it was. That scruffy bit of paper.

You get drunk.
You spend all your money
on yourself.
Thats enough.

I didn't refer to the message for a couple of days. I was scared to. Instead I tried to be a bit more considerate, to pull myself back from my obsession. Finally I could bear it no longer and confronted her with the paper.

"Look darling, I know I've been completely wrapped up with the book, the course and my exams lately. I must be an absolute pain to live with; but I hadn't realised that it had gone this far."

She glanced at the paper. "Oh that. That's just some French phrases that came up when I was talking with Brigitte."

(Brigitte is a French friend of ours. She and Ann used to meet up for conversational practice.)

And then the snow came. It began on a Tuesday, little flakes at first. So beautiful that I opened the shutters and watched it. Then I went out to saw some wood, mesmerised by the silently falling flakes, getting bigger now.

By the time the kids came home, it was a white-out. Intense excitement. Out we all went into the darkness. A free for all snow fight was waged until it was time for tea.

"Hot water bottles all round tonight."

"Thanks, mum!"

"And hot milk for Flavie dog?" Asks David.

"And hot milk for Flavie dog."

But the best was to come in the morning.

Wednesday was a no-school day (Saturday being a half day), so normally it would have been impossible to shift Alice and David much before ten. Today, of course, was different. After kitting the kids up with hats, scarves, boots and coats, it was all outside. Alice had a 'wicked' hat. A combination of hat and scarf that were all the rage at school. We had spent a whole day searching for it in the shops of Avranches.

Next, the pond had to be thawed out so that the birds could drink. Ways and means were discussed.

"Hit it with a hammer."

"No, silly, that would stun the fish."

"Alice is right darling. The shock waves are very great in water. I'll boil up a pan and we'll put it on the ice. That'll melt a hole. Then we can put in a plastic bottle so that it doesn't freeze over again."

"Then can we make a snowman?"

"Great. It must be built by the edge of the garden, looking onto the lane."

"No, it should be just in front of the house."

"Oh yes. I'll get the spades."

"I'll go and look for the sledge."

"That could take some time."

We had wondered whether to bring the sledge, thinking that we were unlikely to have snow in France. *Bien sur*, I had no idea where it was. Was it in the attic? The lean-to? Eventually I ran it to earth sitting up in the rafters in the barn. It hadn't been used for years, so I got to work waxing the runners with my candle wax.

I don't suppose everybody has a hundredweight bag of candle wax, but I've hauled mine around with me for thirty years, since I was a kid at school in the sixties and I used to make my own candles, watching the different colours running into each other while listening to Spooky Tooth, or Caravan, or Pink Floyd, or Zodiac Cosmic Sounds (in the dark, as recommended on the cover). Significant man.

Except for the occasional caw of a rook, it was perfectly still, perfectly silent. It was as if we were in a painting by Bruegel. The snow continued to fall. We carried the sledge down the road to René's field by the stream. Under the banks, we knew that the muskrats would be sleeping out the winter in their holes. On this steep slope, the trick would be to stop before hitting the water!

"I want to be on the front."

"No, me."

"No, no, me. You were allowed to put the carrot in the snowman!"

Pulling the sledge up to the top of the hill. Launching the children down the slope. Having a running snowball fight between times. Flavie, young puppy as she was, going crazy in the snow, chasing her tail. Barking wildly.

Being ambushed by the kids. Snow down the back of my neck. Trying to get them to fight each other, but ending up as the main target. As always.

Ann stalking me with a snowball. Me running. She throws it. It misses. I scoop up some snow and chase her. Closer. Closer. She can't get away. Surely I can't be about to throw it at her at this range? I throw the snow away. Grab her round the waist and kiss her.

"Thank God for that!"

"You didn't really think I was going to throw it at you from that distance, did you?"

"No, it's not that. It's the first time I've seen you smile for weeks."

Looking at my wife. A return to sanity.

SELLING FRENCH DREAMS

SANGLIER

Monsieur Bernard. Boarish behaviour.
A French small farm. The Citroen has its uses.

As winter drew towards spring, I once again turned my attention to house hunting. Having built up a catalogue of over a hundred houses for my first employer, I now had to take on a similar number for my second one. I rang up a couple of the notaires who I had worked with before, but not surprisingly they weren't willing to play ball. Their agreement was with the agency. If I had changed agency, that agreement was at an end. I was back to the same point that I had been many months earlier. Once again, I took to putting 'houses wanted' leaflets on shop notice boards, in bars, and in the letterboxes of houses already up for sale.

One such 'drop' led me to meeting Monsieur ... well, I will call him Monsieur Bernard. In fact I will simply call him Bernard. Bernard was (and is) a small tradesman. I won't say what trade he exercised, or where he lived, for reasons that will become obvious by and by. I will just say that it was a *metier* that meant that he spent a lot of time out and about and that he therefore knew a great number of country people. Among the thousand bits of country news and lore that he carried round in his head, he knew who was selling what property, and where.

Bernard was of medium height and dark. He smoked like a chimney (though not in my car if I could help it) and always wore a slightly hunted look, as though he expected at any moment to be tapped on the shoulder by a *gendarme*. Come to think of it, he probably did.

Bernard was a Breton, and many of the houses that we were to see were on or over the border with Brittany. Like most Bretons, he was passionate about his land, and at first on our journeys I would quiz him about Brittany. I had already learnt a great deal about Normandy from Doctor Marais. The good doctor, as I have recounted elsewhere (in *A Normandy Tapestry*), was afire with both passion for, and knowledge of, Normandy's history, geography, wildlife and people and could hold me spell-bound for hours.

If I hoped to find in Bernard a Breton equivalent of Doctor Marais, I was to be disappointed. Bernard was passionate in his belief that Brittany should be independent from France 'like Wales is from England', but he was not very knowledgeable about the history of his land.

Like many of our beliefs, Bernard's convictions were more founded on what he'd heard on his mother's knee than anything he could have explained rationally. Be that as it may, he inspired in me a great desire to learn more about Brittany, and specifically to go and buy the excellent *Histoire de la Bretagne* (By Yann Brekillien).

His actual complaints about the French state were, apart from one, hardly specific to Brittany. Anywhere in France you can hear the moan that Paris is too centralist and doesn't understand the regions. You can hear much the same in Britain about London; although it must be said that the complaint seems far more justified in France.

The one complaint that Bernard made about Paris which was specific to Brittany, was that the capital thinks continental, while Brittany is a maritime region. As I learned more of Brittany's extraordinary maritime history and culture, I came to entirely agree with him.

The fact that Bernard knew many people with property to sell brought me in a fair number of houses. After I had been out with him a few times to visit single properties, he suggested that we go for an all-day trip and visit several houses in one go. As an immediate payment for his time (he would also get cash on the sale of any houses that he had introduced), he asked only that on the final trip of the day we visited his shooting cabin in the woods to pick something up.

What it was that we were to collect, he wouldn't say, except to assure me that it was not to be one of his hunting trophies (I didn't fancy my car looking like a butcher's shop), but it was fragile. That's why he wanted to use my car. His own Citroen, which he normally used for the trip, had a problem with the suspension. The Citroen is, bless it, as prone to 'the old suspension trouble' as an old club-man to gout.

Bernard took me to see five properties that day, ranging in area from the bay of Mont St Michel, right across to the other end of my 'patch', the Forest of Saint Sever. They were the usual mixed bag; two completely unsaleable, one possible, one quite attractive. The final property was a farm below the Forest of Saint Sever.

The forest lies between Vire and Villedieu and is a big and lonely place with many lakes and pools. The land is quite hilly thereabouts, rising to about a thousand feet. The farms are generally on rocky, poor soil and isolated one from another by woods or arms of the forest. The place is criss-crossed by tracks.

Bernard's shooting cabin was in the forest. We were to drive past it (a short-cut) to the farm, then return the same way to pick up his mysterious bundle.

As Bernard was navigating today, I didn't have to worry about map reading, for which I was very grateful. Alas, the gratitude was not to last for long. I've approached houses, barns and ruins by some bad tracks in my time, but Monsieur Bernard's short-cut was appalling.

To begin with it wasn't too bad. Rough, certainly, but not out of the ordinary. That rough initial track ended in an abandoned quarry. It was the way that led out of the quarry which was the shocker. Leading steeply uphill, with wheel ruts far below the centre of the road and partly overgrown, it looked as if it hadn't been travelled for months. I had to put the car on 'super-bounce' almost at once. Not for the first time, I blessed my Citroen (I think I blessed and cursed it in equal measure). I turned to my passenger in some alarm:

"My God, is it like this all the way?"

He smiled at me. "Courage my friend. This is what your car was made for. Not too far now. Besides, can you imagine trying to back out of here?"

He had a point there. I carried on. We went through a wood (startling a deer) and forward. Bracken swished along the wings of the car, while small branches snapped against the windscreen, making me flinch involuntarily. It was like being upstairs on the school bus.

"Your hunting hut is remote enough, Bernard. What do you hunt up here?"

"Oh a few things, according to the season. Hare. Rabbit. Pheasant. Woodcock. Partridge."

At the time, a couple of these words meant nothing to me. I always jotted down words that I didn't understand, usually on the forms I used for property details. When I got home, I would write them up on to my little cardboard cards, with the English translation on the other side.

Whenever I had a spare minute, I would take a dozen of the cards, read the English and write out the French. Then I would turn over the card to check that I was right. If everything was correct, spelling, accents, gender, I would put the card to the back of the pile. If not, I would put it to the front, so that I would come to it first next time. Simple technology, but all of my own invention, and remarkably effective.

"And, *bien sur*," said Bernard with a reverence akin to a Welshman's for rugby, "that most magnificent, that lord of beasts, the *sanglier*."

Ah yes, the boar. I knew that the beast lived in the Saint Sever forest. I had met the 'Lord of the hunt' when I valued his magnificent house some time before, but I knew little about it. Bernard, ecstatically, filled the gap in my knowledge.

"The boar is the king of European beasts. It is the most

111

intelligent animal on the continent and the most exciting to hunt. And that hunting is justified, if further justification were needed, as one must control its population, and to limit the damage it does to crops."

"Ah oui." I remarked cynically (I very nearly said *'ouaii'*, but restrained myself.) "I've noticed that you French can always find perfect justification for shooting off at anything that moves."

"The boar breeds very quickly and is strongly on the increase," he replied, stung by my remark, "how else should we keep the numbers down? How do you control the wild boar in your country?"

"Well actually, it's extinct."

"Vraiment?" He glowered at me.

I changed gear sharply. He had me there perhaps, but it didn't invalidate my comment. The French hunting fraternity contains a very nasty element who will quite happily resort to other tactics when they can't win their way with words. I remembered reading just the week before an article about the Green Party trying to rein back the annual slaughter of migratory birds which had said something like:

"At the issue of another report, the extremists will undoubtedly work up a lather again. Whip up the troops with barefaced lies and throw stones at politicians. The huntsmen apply a scientific rule (a very French one) which can be expressed 'a terrorised M.P. will always defend those who terrorise him.'"

And of course, as the article said, that doesn't just apply to huntsmen.

Bernard was off again:
"You generally find them in forests with clearings and thick

cover, and of course they must have water. Dense bramble thickets suit them well. Having said that, you can just as easily find them lying up in ferns at the bottom of an old oak tree, or in the rushes at the tail of a lake. When the corn and maize come into fruit, he'll take to the fields. Then he'll lie up in the mud of the irrigation ditches. He loves wallowing in the mud. It keeps him cool and keeps the flies and ticks off."

The track bumped along. A stone clanged somewhere beneath us. I wasn't surprised his car was out of action.

"They have a matriarchal society. A herd will have three or four sows. The oldest and most experienced is in charge, leading the group about, including the young males. The young of both sexes do everything together, eating, moving, sleeping. They are very affectionate animals who love to be close and pile on top of each other when they sleep."

I smiled. I was beginning to feel quite a warmth for the wood-pig that Bernard was describing.

"As they get older, the young males become more and more solitary. When the rut starts, the rutting boar will evict them all - they'll be twelve to eighteen months old by then - from the herd."

"*Ah oui.*" I grunted. But my companion needed no encouragement.

"Then the young boars form small unstable groups. It's those groups that do most harm to the crops, because they're not cautious like their elders. They get into the fields and lie up in the ditches, like I said earlier. They cause tremendous damage. When they get to four or five years old, the males split-up and live alone. Look, the hut's up there."

We had come to a fork in the track.

"Carry on to the left. We'll come back this way."

"If I have any suspension."

Bernard laughed. "You must learn to trust Monsieur Citroen."

"And the boar?"

"Ah yes, the boar. Normally the rut starts in December, unless it's been a very good year, in which case it can start a bit earlier. The old boars leave their lairs and travel sometimes great distances looking for sows to cover."

"The chief sow comes into heat first. She'll mark the trees so that the boar can find her. When the boar comes into the group, he chases off, as I mentioned, the young boars. If two boars meet, they'll fight it out. They can wound each other badly, although it's rarely fatal. Ah here we are. I'll get out and open the gate. The farm is just over there on the right."

We had come out of the trees now. It was a very still and sunny day. Bernard opened the sagging gate with difficulty and I drove out on to what I would normally have considered a poorish track; but which seemed like a motorway compared to the one we'd just left.

Next, we drove through a boggy meadow, the watercourse carrying the green stalks of the iris flags that would bloom everywhere in yellow millions in the summer. There, beyond an orchard of apple trees, was our destination - the Vignerons' farm. It was an attractive group of buildings.

I drove up, parked the car and took the key out of the ignition. I didn't do this out of any sense of concern for security but because the car, perhaps because she (*voiture* being, of course, feminine) is French, is a temperamental beast. I have left the key in and shut the doors on her before and she has rewarded me by closing down the central locking, leaving me locked outside and the key inside. I suspected that she might be feeling even huffier than usual after Bernard's short-cut.

A little distance away, pitching muck into the back of his trailer, was Monsieur Vigneron. He nodded at Bernard, offered me the back of his hand (the palms were filthy, but there must always be a handshake on meeting, even if it has to be as stylised as this).

"My wife's inside. I'll join you in a minute."

Madame Vigneron greeted us warmly and offered me the inevitable coffee and calvados.

"Come, I'll show you around."

Although just about every rural property that I visited cast its magic round me; the stone walled houses, the great slate-roofs, the dark and rustic interiors, the attics and cellars, the barns, the hoary old orchards, the flower-choked lanes, the meandering streams, the wells, this was quite the most engaging place that I had ever visited. Partly it was because it had the life of a couple. Many of the farms that I visited were empty or lived in by only a farmer or (more generally) his widow. This house was bustling, energetic, well-painted and clean as a new pin.

They kept cows, a bull, a couple of pigs, chickens. There were a few geese and several ducks on the pond. A couple of fields were laid down to crops; apparently maize. Everything was in fine heart, and well looked after.

Finally, details taken, we ended up back in the kitchen, where we sat on benches at the big scrubbed table. The Vignerons talked about their life. They had two sons. Both had left the farm. Did they not want to carry on the family business?

Monsieur Vigneron scowled.

"No, they've too much brains for that. Why slave your life away 365 days a year. Out in the fields whatever the weather, whatever the season. Up to your neck in muck. *Non, Monsieur, le jeu n'en vaut pas la chandelle.*" (Literally, the game's not worth the candle). He brushed a bluebottle away with his hand:

"Then there's the red tape. Forms, forms, forms. And

where does it get you? I'd get more if I was on the SMIC (dole). Why bother with all that when you can get a nice nine to five job and take your five weeks holiday a year?"

"We're not moving far," volunteered his wife, "up to Lessay, you know, where the horse fair is. We'll miss the old place. It's given us some good times; and some rough ones too. It doesn't do to be too sentimental, but you can't weigh a life by the money it brings. And it's not just work here, it's our life."

"It certainly looks as if you've put a lot of love into the place." I said admiringly.

"Maybe the English gentleman would like to buy the farm himself?" Bernard put in. I noticed that his cigarette had a long cone of ash on it.

"Ah," I said, "Houses are like women. You can admire them, but it's safest to keep to one at a time." I heard myself say it as if I was going through an out-of-body experience. Had I been possessed by a Frenchman?

They laughed. I was a little embarrassed. Then I broached the subject of the price of the property. The farmer shrugged. "Of course, the place is up for sale with my notaire. It has already been valued by him. The price is 320,000 francs, *à debattre un peu.*" (with a bit of leeway).

I said nothing. About £30,000. In British terms it was absurdly cheap; the same price for a working farm as for a terraced house in an inexpensive part of England. The farm would sell quickly, I could sell it myself five times over. With its sale an era would end. It would be a holiday home.

I sat at the kitchen table writing out the details. I had mixed feelings about selling-off small farms. Not about selling to second home owners. Outside buyers, foreigners no less than French, are seen as a positive thing in the French countryside. Certainly this is the case in Normandy, where the population of many communes has halved since the war. If outsiders didn't buy the property it would simply fall down and have no value at all. Just as obviously, the new owners, be they British, German or French (the French themselves having three million *maisons secondaires*) would doubtless love the Vigneron farm and treat it sympathetically.

But I was saddened to see the death of a lifestyle, and there is no doubt that that is what's happening to traditional French agriculture. As at the year 2001, ninety farms a day disappear in France. In the last forty years, seven out of ten French farms have gone.

And with ever fewer and ever bigger farms, the landscape too is changing. Large chunks of Brittany have already had the 'Norfolk treatment', where the age-old pattern of hedgerows and banks have been torn out to make mega-fields. Pray to God that the same thing does not happen in the *bocage*.

Finished! I rearranged my papers, put the top back on my pen and rose to leave the Vigneron farm.

So we set off back towards Bernard's *cabane* in the woods. As anticipated, it was even worse getting up to the place than the journey out had been, for the final hundred yards were mostly tree roots and ferns. The cabin was a modest wooden affair, padlocked and shuttered.

Bernard unlocked the door, ushered me in and undid the shutters. There wasn't a lot to see. A wood stove, a table, some chairs, a fishing rod, a couple of traps. I had meant to ask him more about boars, but, after asking me to wait and assuring me that he would not be long, he left me to my own devices.

On the wall hung an old *Elle et Vire* agricultural calendar.

Each day had its saint listed against it. I noticed that today was Saint Gontran's day. On the table were the corpses of two butterflies.

I picked up the only bit of literature in the place. The *Annuaire des fabricants de matériel pour la chasse au sanglier* - a catalogue of manufacturers' equipment for boar hunting. A title that you would be unlikely to see in W.H. Smiths. I opened it idly. There were clothes, binoculars, boots (fourteen makes. Very keen on their *bottes* are the French), knives, night-sights and rifles a-plenty. Looking through that lot, I could readily see why the 'sportsmen' succeed in bagging a goodly number of their own kind (and innocent by-standers) each year.

I had been entertaining myself in this manner for a minute or two when Bernard re-appeared. He was smoking a cigarette and was wreathed in smoke.

"All done. I've got them together. We can put them in the car now."

"Them?" I growled. "What? I told you, no corpses, and preferably no machine-guns, land mines, hand grenades or collapsible gallows either."

He laughed nervously. "No, nothing like that. Just some jars."

Jars? Pickled gherkins? Was he bottling walnuts or whinberries? "You'd better show me then."

I followed him out to the car. There on the ground were ten one-gallon (or the French equivalent thereof) jars, each full to the brim with yellow liquid.

"Calvados?"

He nodded. "*Ouaii, Eau-de-vie de cidre.* You know, I bring it down from here now and again, but it takes a car with good suspension. Or else the jars might break." He ended lamely.

I could see exactly where he was coming from. Bernard

was distilling moonshine somewhere out back and was asking me to transport it out of the woods for him.

"And just what is the penalty for shifting booze about; should the not-impossible come to pass and one is stopped by the law?"

It was far from being an unlikely event. The police in rural France are apparent in a way that they are not in England. Whereas at home I have only once been stopped by the police in over twenty years, in France it happened every second week.

"That's not very likely, *Monsieur Bee-geen*. You are an Englishman. They won't bother you."

He was right. When they heard my accent and my (deliberately) broken French, the *gendarmes* had always given up in disgust, not even bothering to press me for my documents (which was just as well, as I never carried them with me).

"*Ouaii,* (I couldn't stop myself from saying it) I'll tell the magistrate you said that."

"*Monsieur Bee-geen,*" he began, then hesitated and tried a different tack: "Alain." He wheedled. "I have just remembered some properties down Courtils way that are on the market, and my wife's aunt's brother-in-law has got a couple of places near Dol de Bretagne which he wants to dispose of. He knows lots of people down there, practically everyone....."

Dol de Bretagne? A new area. It was true that if you met one seller it often led to others. "O.K." I shrugged. "You've persuaded me to join the black market. "And put that bloody fag out before you get in my car."

Together, we carefully put the bottles in the boot, separating them with newspaper.

We did pass a policeman on the way back to Bernard's, but

although he looked closely at me (or so it seemed to my perhaps over-sensitive imagination), he didn't flag us down.

My friend must have noticed that I was relieved to see the back of his bottles. He patted me gently on the shoulder. "You worry too much, *Alain*. Perhaps you should take a holiday."

"Thanks Bernard. As a matter of fact, we are going away. I had meant to tell you. I won't be around next week."

"*Ah bon? Où vas-tu?*"

"To Brittany, funnily enough, but in the south. We're staying with some friends down there."

"Then you're sure to have a good time. Think of me in the evenings when you are drinking your *calva*."

"I will, Bernard, I will."

Thus ended my first brush with French law. I did not realise that soon I was to have a much more serious one.

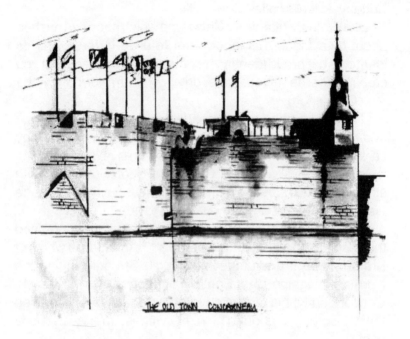

THE OLD TOWN CONCARNEAU.

Into Brittany. On the beach.
<u>Day Walk!</u> A fine night.

We are on holiday in Brittany.

Brittany is the only one of the six Celtic regions which is not in the British Isles. That is, of course, no coincidence. The Bretons originated in Great Britain (Grande Bretagne) and fled to Brittany (Petite Bretagne) to escape the Anglo-Saxon invaders in the sixth century. That explains why so many Breton place names, Trelaze, Saint Renan, Lannion and so on, could easily be in Cornwall. Indeed, there is an area of Brittany which is called Cournaille.

Like Wales, Brittany is a Celtic land which has been pushed about by a bigger neighbour, but refuses to foreswear its identity. That proud identity becomes obvious as soon as you cross the border (in our case, driving in from Normandy, the river Cousenon).

The road-signs are suddenly in two languages. The black and white striped Breton flag is everywhere to be seen. Many cars carry the Breton plaque, 'BZH' (it has always puzzled me why some of those other Celts, the Scots, carry *Ecosse* stickers on their cars. To declare your nationality in someone else's language seems an odd thing to do).

The Bretons have had to struggle for their language and their flag (union with France was in 1532). Indeed the whole of Breton history is a catalogue of struggle. Struggle against the Normans, against the English and against the French. Consequently, the land is covered with castles and fortified towns. Romantic enough now, but witness to a very bloody past.

But there is more, far more, to this Celtic land than the story of old wars. The 'matter' of Brittany is the sea. With three thousand kilometres of coast, this is perhaps not surprising. To quote from *the History of Brittany*:

> 'The prow of the great ship of Europe, it
> thrusts into the ocean which howls and tears
> at its flanks, exhaling on its granite highlands
> a breath charged with ozone and clouds.'

Nor is it surprising that the Bretons are much the most maritime of the French peoples (if I may dare to call them that). The ferries which ply between Britain and France are often

Brittany Ferries. Jaques Cartier, 'discoverer' of Canada was a Breton (sorry about the inverted commas. It's just that I'm pretty sure that the locals already knew the place was there).

Sailors and fishermen from Saint Malo gave the Falkland Isles their Spanish name of *Malvinas* and the French one, *Les Malouines*. A disproportionate number of Bretons have always served in the French navy. And, like the Irish, Bretons have traditionally emigrated to find work; to Canada, New York and Paris.

If the sea is central to the great tale of Brittany, it is also essential to the tiny tale of our family holiday there. That holiday takes place near Lorient, where we are sharing a rented cottage with our friends, Colin and Sue, and their children, Katie and Peter.

Today, we are on the beach. The sands are perfect and the sun is shining from a clear sky. Towels have been laid and cool-bags have been placed in what shade we can find or create. We are in our swimming togs.

It is a perfect day for lilos and books, sun-cream and dozing, and perhaps an occasional dip in the sea. But there is little chance of that. As any parent of small children knows, you can forget such civilized pleasures for a few years.

We are to make a bathing pool. To do this, we must dam-up the small streams which run through the sands. Ann, Sue and the kids will make the dam. Colin and I are stone-gatherers. The children are not about to let us become lazy, indeed the devil seems to have got into them today:

"Come on, Uncle Colin. There's a breach here. Find a bigger stone!"

"More stones dad, more stones!"

Soon, other children arrive and help our wives with the dam (we usually end up with other peoples' kids as well as our own; but never mind, we like kids). This frees up our four kids for the task of making their own Breton megalithic constructions. We visited Carnac yesterday, that most mysterious of ancient sites, and they are alive with megalith madness.

"More stones dad! More stones Uncle Alan! We need to start on the dolmens and menhirs!"

The boys are in charge of dolmen construction. The word 'Dolmen' is taken (in a slightly dodgy way) from the Welsh/ Breton for stone table (men = stone), which means that it is the construction where two or more stones are used to hold up a capping stone. They were used for individual or mass burials. Bone stores - ossuaries - which, when full, may have simply been emptied and the process begun again (also the custom in Breton churches until the nineteenth century).

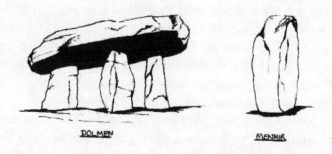

DOLMEN   MENHIR

The girls are in charge of menhirs. 'Menhir' simply means standing stone. Many suggestions have been made for their use, from markers to ley lines. Folklore says that they were put up as spots where the spirit could linger for seven years before being reborn in the body of a baby. On some of them, in some lights, carved faces can be seen. Spooky.

These standing stones occur in enormous groups and often in regular shapes, such as the straight lines that we saw at Carnac, which stretch for several kilometres and number more than a thousand stones.

Colin and I are finding it hard to keep up with the demands of our megalith crew. Carrying the stones to the dam is getting more difficult. We've exhausted the supply of small rocks over a wide area. We're carrying big or we're carrying far. We should have realised that we were likely to have problems from the talk we were given at Carnac about the originals.

How these mammoth stones were placed is a mystery. Fine, stones of twenty or thirty tons could have been rolled, but for those of hundreds of tons? For example, the grand menhir of Locmariaquer was sixty five feet high and weighed three hundred and fifty tons (it's in four bits now).

The capping stones of the dolmens of Mané Lud, Mané Rutual and the Table des Marchands are almost equally massive. They couldn't have been moved by wooden levers: they would have sheared. Similarly, if you tried to roll blocks like that, the weight would simply drive the rollers into the ground. The supporting stones are often embedded mere inches into the ground and yet somehow they were balanced and after five or six thousand years they're still there.

And if the raising of the standing stones is a mystery, then so is the way that the builders aligned those stones and barrows with the underground water table. An isolated Menhir is generally situated above the spot where an underground stream divides into two or three. Dolmens are also often associated with water. At Locmariaquer the paved alley exactly follows the course of an underground stream.

Of course, Brittany is only one of the places where these mysterious stone pillars, circles, avenues and dolmens occur. They are scattered all along the Atlantic seaboard from Jutland to Spain, as well as throughout the Western Isles of Scotland, in Wales, Ireland and on both sides of the Channel. My favourite is called 'Blue man 'i the moss' and is on my own beloved Yorkshire moors (A corruption of a Celtic name, needless to say: 'Blue man' = *plu maen* = *boundary stone*). But the greatest of all of these constructions are to be found in England, in Wiltshire: Stonehenge and Silbury.

The remarkable thing about the Breton stones is how immensely old they are. Scientific dating using carbon fourteen have shown that they predate the first Egyptian pyramids by a thousand years.

"More stones dad! More stones Uncle Colin!" They chirrup angrily like a nest of hungry chicks.

A topless woman walks past through the waves. Colin and I stop. Our heads swivel round.

Sex. Of course that universal impulse is present in the standing stones. Where the spirits lingered waiting to be born, girls would come to seek them. Which explains the Breton custom, prevalent until the last century, and it is rumoured existent even now (another example of a rebirth?), of girls passing the night on a dolmen, or rubbing themselves naked against a menhir to attract the waiting souls into their bodies.

As I drag a particularly large boulder to the edge of the now impressive bathing pool, Ann stands up.

"Come on," she says, "I've had enough of this. We're going on strike. Time for a swim."

Ignoring the protests of the children (slave drivers!), we run into the sea. Run, run until we are up to our knees then throw ourselves forward. A wave crashes over us. Laughing and spluttering, we strike out for deeper water.

According to *The History of Brittany*, below and before us, choked by reeds and weeds, full five fathoms deep and bells a-tolling, may lie fabled Atlantis herself. But that's another story...

Wonderful, beautiful, mysterious Brittany.

Escape! We dreamt about it on the beach yesterday. Today's the day we make the break! Colin and I are going on our day walk!

I've been going on long walks since I was in the R.A.F, which I joined when I was seventeen. Then, the walks were rather grandiosely termed 'Expedition Training'. The Armed Forces go out of their way to keep their people fit for obvious reasons. As far as we airmen and airwomen were concerned the rationale didn't matter a lot, as long as we could pile into a canvas-topped three-ton truck and head up the A1 to the Peak District, or the Lakes, and spend a couple of days out (with a stop at a transport café on the way for sausage egg and chips, a slice of bread and butter and a cup of tea). Heaven!

When I came out of the Air Force (at the age of twenty-one), I continued to love a decent walk. I got a few mates interested and we used to go out most weekends up into the Chiltern Hills. Guys 'n gals walking fifteen to twenty miles and drinking Brakspear's beer ('The Shakespeare of beers' - my slogan, not theirs). We called ourselves 'The Gunslingers' (after a poem by Edward Dorn).

Several times a year we would go further afield, to Snowdonia, the Peaks, Dartmoor, the Brecons. The major difference from when I was in the Air Force was that now the Government wasn't paying.

Since the kids came along, there hasn't been much time for walking, or rather when there has, it has been with one (or exceptionally both) of them on my shoulders. That's wonderful too; but not a proper walk. <u>Today will be a proper walk!</u>

We packed the day-sack yesterday evening. All the necessary stuff is in there. Sandwiches, a couple of bars of chocolate, some cake, two apples, an orange which - if past experience is anything to go by - will never get eaten, but will be discovered, dried up and shrunken, in six months time. Spare socks, cagoule (waterproof jacket) and over-trousers (Colin is a magnet for rain. There should be an entry for him in the Met. Report. Dogger, Fisher, German Bight and Colin).

We are dressed in shorts and T-shirts. I have a map and compass about my person (rather fetchingly swinging from my belt and now and then clacking comfortingly against my thigh). Colin has the day-sack. We will take turns with map reading and carrying the sack, hour on, hour off.

Today we're walking up the River Scorff. We're about twenty miles upriver from Lorient, where the river flows into the Atlantic. Lorient. A nice practical name: l'orient, the east. It was founded as the port where supplies were shipped from France for the French East India company. Until Britain pinched India off them. Now it's home to the fishing fleet of the supermarket *Intermarché.* Imagine, a supermarket having its own fishing fleet.

We've planned our route carefully. There are plenty of paths in France; some of them are *Grandes Randonnées* - long distance footpaths, although there don't seem to be any *Petites Randonnées* - i.e. workaday footpaths; but there are lots of tracks, and anyway the law of access is rather kinder in France than it is in England.

We're wildly happy. Today is escape. Escape from work.

Escape from wives. Escape from children. (This isn't as selfish as it may seem. Tomorrow we'll look after the kids and the womenfolk get to escape; though why they would want to get away from such perfect husbands as Colin and I is a bit of a mystery).

I'm like Mr Toad with his new car. Everything is out there, just waiting to be found: fish and fowl, that which goes on four legs and that which squirms on its belly. Woods, forests, fields, flowers, gardens, glades and all that is green. Geography, geology, the sea and the sky. Man and all his works: customs and eccentricities, habits and history, castles and cathedrals, *villes* and villages. Characters! Adventure! Everything.

We would have preferred to have a 'Blue' map (1 to 25,000 or 2.5 inches to the mile), which even show field boundaries, or one of the 'Brown' series (1 to 50,000). But these are devilishly difficult to get hold of, so we have had to settle for one of the 'Green' series maps (1 to 100,000. 1cm to 1km). These aren't great for walking, but they're all we could get; and anyway it's a straightforward enough route: along a minor road to a village, onto the river bank, follow the river for seven miles, then back on the other side by another minor road.

And so Colin parks his car, we put on our boots and stride out. The first stretch to the village is fairly uneventful. Up and down a hill. We don't notice it that much. Colin is telling me about his brother Bob's latest escapades. Bob's a character, best known, perhaps, for carrying a wardrobe up the Pennine Way, long before lugging fridges through Ireland became a craze. Before we know it, we are in the couple of deserted streets that make up the village.

"That looks suspiciously like a bar opposite the church."

"At ten o'clock in the morning, Al?"

"Well, we are on holiday. And it's the only bar we'll see

today."

"Oh go on then. Just a quick one. There's a table on the pavement, so we can sit outside."

Colin and I are of a piece. We can resist anything but temptation (thank you Oscar).

"*Monsieur*?"

Colin orders two beers.

"A fine day, *messieurs*," offers the *patron*.

"*Il va pleuvoir plus tard*." I rejoin.

"Rain later? *Mais, non Monsieur*. It's lovely."

I don't say anything. If the 'Colin Effect' isn't understood in Brittany, I'm not going to enlighten them.

We walk through into the adjoining shop (same *patron*) and buy a couple of things: some crisps, a piece of goat's cheese.

"You're walking today?"

"Yes, that's right."

"Then it's a pity I've run out of *Andouille*." The *patron* looks sad. "That would have gone down well with your meal."

"Oh yes," I agree. "What a shame"

"Never mind," he brightens up, "there's a good place for *andouille* not far from here. At Guémené-sur-Scorff."

"That's very kind. We'll bear it in mind. Bit far for a day walk, unfortunately."

We take our beers and sit in the sun. They don't last long and I'm soon back for more. The *patron* is a friendly man and we are his only customers. I tell him that we are walking up the River Scorff.

"You are interested in the fishing perhaps?"

"No, we're not fishermen. Is it a good river?"

"Superb. You get trout here and lampreys - all three species, the river lamprey, the little lamprey and the great sea lamprey, that can grow up to a metre long - and eels. Then of course there is," his voice drops reverently, *"le saumon."*

"Salmon?"

"Oh yes, the Scorff is renowned for its salmon. The stocks are very well managed."

"Vraiment?"

"Ah oui," he leans slightly across the bar to pass me the drinks. "What a creature! They leave the river when they're a couple of years old and swim the Atlantic Ocean all the way across to Greenland. The astonishing power of life, sir! But they always come back to their own river to spawn. They say that they can tell their birthing waters by their smell. That again is incredible! Consider, the thousands of currents that flow .....oh, excuse me, *Monsieur.*"

The dictatorial demand of a telephone breaks in on this - to me - totally fascinating story. I hurry out to Colin with the beers and tell him of our conversation.

"Then we'd better get on, buddy boy. I can't wait to see the Scorff."

"Yes, best make a move before the rain starts."

Colin grunts good-naturedly. We leave payment on the table and move on.

The Scorff is a beautiful river. Its bed is granite, with outcrops of (I think) mica and feldspar glistening here and there. Small islands stand out in the stream. It is shallow (though there are what look like very deep pools under the banks), not too wide and, at the moment, moving slowly. Woods slope down to the river.

We walk along in silence for a while, enchanted by the scenery. Suddenly, Colin stops. I nearly crash into him. "See it?" As Colin is long-sighted and a bit of an ornithologist, I assume he has seen a bird.

"There!" He grabs my arm and points. I am short-sighted

131

and therefore not an ornithologist at all. I see nothing.

"There, again!"

"Sorry mate."

"A kingfisher!"

The kingfisher is a bird that I often don't see.

It's getting on for mid-day now. We stop to reconnoitre the ruins of an old mill, clambering through a wrecked window to look inside. The place is choked with nettles and rubble. It is rather sad. Once this was the home of a family, with children and a thousand tales. Now the spirit has fled.

We carry on past the ruined weir and along the river bank. The river widens-out here and becomes shallower. By taking a great leap and then scrambling from boulder to boulder, we reach a couple of big slabs of rock, nearly in midstream. We get out our sandwiches and lie in the sun.

"What are *andouilles*?" asks Colin.

"You don't want to know. Not suitable for the English."

He reflects on this as he settles himself comfortably on the rock. "This is the life. We haven't seen any salmon though."

"I think the Celts regard it as sacred."

"I don't suppose that stops them eating them."

"No, I don't suppose it does."

He closes his eyes. Colin has a genius for cat-napping. I wake him up twenty minutes later. A leech has fastened itself to his leg, proving that he does have his attractions after all. He's lucky that it wasn't a lamprey. He gets it off by applying the lighted end of one of my cigars to its rear elevation. Until now, the only advantage that I had known of for my nicotine addiction was that apparently cannibals hate to eat smokers. Now I realise that there is more to the habit than that.

"Better get on, boy. Have you seen the sky?"

"Cheeky sod. I was waiting for you."

We set off again. It is getting on for two p.m. and we are anxiously looking out for the bridge where we will cross the Scorff and turn for home. The sky darkens. And darkens again. The first heavy drops of rain fall. The 'Colin Effect' has arrived. Dead on time. Exactly mid-point in our journey.

We turn a corner. There! There, ahead, the bridge! We run for its shelter as the storm tears the heavens apart. Under the bridge, a vivid green patch of duckweed is trapped behind some twigs.

This storm means business. Ahead of us, lightning cracks from sky to ground. Crash! Craash! Craaash! The thunder is getting nearer. We try to work out how near. What is it, four seconds between the lightning and the thunder means a mile; or is it five seconds? What's the speed of sound?

"Cake, old pal?"

"I reckon."

We open the plastic container and get out the cake. Fruit cake. Fabulous. We bless our wives. The bridge isn't very wide, but the rain is falling so straight that there is enough shelter nonetheless. It boils off the river in a mist, a cloud hanging before our eyes. The river hisses like a thing alive; it is rising as we watch. The twigs and duckweed float downstream, an iridescent yellow-green stain on the muscle of the surging flood.

In the end, it is obvious that the rain isn't going to stop. We put on our cagoules, though we're not sure that there's much point really. It is so warm that we will steam inside the plastic. We'll get wet whatever happens. We don't care too much. There is a savagery, an exhilaration, in this pounding, bouncing water which flows in great torrents alongside the road and sometimes across it. Spring madness. By the time we get back to the car we are completely soaked.

Colin has taken off his glasses because they are worse than useless in this deluge. His hair is plastered against his face and water is running through his beard. He doesn't care. He's grinning like an idiot. He puts out a hand.

"Nice one, eh, Al?" My friend has always been one of life's enthusiasts. Sometimes that's intensely irritating. Sometimes, as now, it puts me to shame.

I grasp the hand. "Nice one, Colin."

When we get home, we are not greeted like the conquering heroes that we undoubtedly are. The girls have lit the stove. There is a comfortable fug. The kids are playing scrabble and hardly notice us. Sue bursts out laughing:

"What are these creatures which seem not of this world and yet are on't?"

Colin frowns. "Best put the kettle on," he says.

It's been a good week. We've been to lots of places. The kids are busy writing it all up in their diary. We've been to a centre for the study of bees and ants. We've been to Le Faouet with its covered market, where we heard Natalie play her Breton bagpipes while the children of the village performed a traditional dance (a somewhat protracted pleasure). We have visited the chapel of St-Fiacre with its wonderful carved rood screen. We've been from Corncarneau to the Isles of Glénan and swum from perfect beaches in the aquamarine sea.

We've been to Lorient, to the great submarine base at Keroman with its massive U-boat pens. This was the largest and most complex of the Atlantic submarine bases which the Germans (or rather their slave labourers) constructed during the war. The Wolf Packs that sailed from Keroman were a terrifying and efficient force which nearly brought Britain to her knees, the seven most successful submarines sinking three hundred and twenty ships between them.

We've played a lot of boules and seen snakes and lizards. We've played scrabble until we think routinely in terms of how many points a word is worth. We've played cribbage and cards. Alice has impressed us all with her 'new magic show'. The kids have organised, and roped us into, their own 'Breton games'. Colin has been most efficient with his handling of the barbecue. We've drunk a lot of wine and eaten a lot of food.

It's been a good week, but tomorrow it is time to leave. We're cheesed off with tidying up. Tonight we are going out to a restaurant.

The restaurant is about a mile away down a very quiet track. We pass just one building on the way; a great deserted granite farmhouse with a lot of outbuildings that we all admire. We see not a single person or car during our walk.

At the restaurant I make my usual mistake of ordering steak which is, *bien sur*, served up almost raw. I send it back. "*Non, bien, bien cuit.*" The waiter looks at me in astonishment. It doesn't seem to make a lot of difference. What I should have said to him really was:

"No lad, don't just pass it over your cigarette lighter. Fry it for twelve hours on Gas Mark twenty!" (if such an instruction is culinarily feasible) to get the compromise five minutes which was needed. We chew (some harder than others) over the events of the week and 'have a bit of a giggle.'

"I saw you looking at that woman on the beach," says Sue to Colin.

"Yes, he was, wasn't he?" I agree.

Colin hangs his head in mock shame.

"So were you dad."

"Nonsense boy," I tell my over-talkative son, "Eat up your

greens!"

We linger long over our meal and polish off several bottles.

When finally we leave, night has fallen. It is a clear moonless night and the stars are out in their infinite millions. So thick they are, arcing above our head, that we see the Milky Way, literally like luminous milk thrown across the blackness, glowing so strong that, when our eyes become accustomed to it, we find that we do not need our torches.

We wander along the road weaving from side to side. Partly with the adults it is 'the drink taken'. Partly it is because we are constantly looking above us, speculating on the constellations, the stars and the planets. Orion's belt. The Plough. The Great Nebula. Andromeda. The Pole Star. Is that Mars?

We think the things which all men and women in all ages who have looked at the heavens have doubtless thought. Who are we, what are we, tiny things in this vast firmament?

As we walk along, we become aware of other lights too. Bright lights from the banks by the roads. The cold yellow fire of countless glow worms. We approach them, but they blink out as we get near.

This is a magical night.

It's been a week of wonders and mysteries. But the greatest of them all is this night of lights in the darkness. We walk slowly and talk in hushed, excited tones.

High in the dome above our head, a speck of light falls away from the million, million lights around it and falls towards the earth.

"A shooting star!" says Katie

"Wow," says Peter.

Wow!

MARCHAND DE BIENS

Marchand de biens.
Putting a damper on things.
Paris Underground. La Défense.

The telephone rang on the stroke of nine. I was sitting right next to it, sorting out a box of papers from the attic. Structured systems analysis and design. Database design. Old computer programs.

"*Allo! C'est moi.*"

"Bernard? What do you want?"

He wanted to show me a house. Bernard had shown me a lot of houses of late. I think that he felt himself in my debt after the calvados incident. At any rate, he had been largely instrumental in helping me build my property portfolio back up to the dizzy heights of one hundred. Together, we visited town houses in Avranches, St James and Dol de Bretagne, village houses in the bay of Mont St Michel and country houses in southern Normandy and northern Brittany.

Some, as ever, were wholly unsuitable. Some of Bernard's acquaintances obviously thought the gullible English (the French invariably referred to anyone from Britain as 'Anglais' and ninety nine percent of our customers were) would buy any rubbish. There was, for example, a concrete shell of a house next to the sea. This was a most odd place. The owner had started to build it and then presumably (and wisely in my opinion) thought better of it. Why he'd built a house without windows was one of life's little mysteries.

When Bernard rang, I hesitated. Today I was going to Paris. But, as I didn't have to catch the train until one o'clock, and the house was quite near Villedieu, where I was to catch the train, I went with him to view 'Old man Druand's house'.

Bernard filled me in about Monsieur Druand as we drove along. He had been a bit of a lad in his time, so it appeared. He had made a fair amount of money at this and that: Bernard didn't want to go into the details. Anyway, wherever Monsieur Druand's money had come from, it was now a matter between him and God, for he had passed on. His nephew from Paris had inherited his house.

Bernard tapped me on the knee. "Well, it's not exactly Old Man Druand's house which is up for sale. That's a fine place - a veritable mansion with a sweeping drive." He ruminated a second. "Posh. The nephew wants to keep that for himself as a *maison secondaire*, his toe in the country to escape from Paris in August."

I chuckled. "So many people escape from Paris in August that the place is practically deserted. If they want peace and quiet, they might be better off staying at home."

Bernard grunted. "Parisians!" He made the word sound almost like a curse. "Sod them. Anyway, what the nephew doesn't want, and this is where you come in, Alain, is the little house that came with the main one. *C'est petite*. However, it has a bit of land with it, and a nice orchard."

"And no calvados?"

"*Ah, non.*"

Bernard guided me to the property. A metalled track - mercifully, this time it was a good one - led up to a house in the middle of an orchard. It was indeed a little place. Free standing, rose-granite as usual, with a slate roof. One up and two down, with a barn on the end. I suppose the external dimensions of the place were about twenty five feet by twelve. It came with five acres of woodlands, ferns and fields - the size of a small park in England. The place was on sale for about ten thousand pounds.

What made it interesting was that the owner, so Bernard said, would accept considerably less. Five thousand pounds, maybe four. He didn't particularly need the money - he was a dammed Parisian wasn't he - he just wanted to get shot of the place. It had been on the notaire's books for a year now. Who would want to buy a titchy place like that?

This was one of those astonishing bargains which one occasionally saw when a house was for sale only with a notaire who didn't take too much interest in selling property. For one reason or another - lack of advertising, or a poor filing system perhaps - a property which had been good value to start with had failed to sell. The owner wanted to be rid of the place and so, unaware that the fault lay more with his notaire than with the price he was asking, he lowered that price to a ludicrous level. I was quite certain that the *petite maison* could have had had no British visitor. It would have been snapped up on sight.

For the cost of a not particularly expensive second-hand car, one could buy a very pretty house and a mini-farm. The house might be small but it had potential. The barn was the key to that. Incorporating it into the house would allow two, maybe three, bedrooms. The structure was excellent and the roof was good. As I've said, such bargains didn't appear too often. It would make an ideal *Marchand de Biens*.

The *Marchand de Biens* is an illustration of how utterly different the French property system is from the British one. French people tend not to move much. That's not surprising when they can expect to pay a hefty whack to the government for the privilege of doing so, and high commission fees on top of that.

So, a few years back, in an attempt to kick-start the market, the government brought in the legal status of *Marchand de Biens* (literally dealer in real estate).

How a M.D.B. operates is that one sets up a Limited Company (SARL) as a M.D.B. and buy and sell a property (or properties) through it. This affords very significant tax advantages. Reg, my new employer, had briefed me on all this. His agency had already 'done an MDB' on several houses, and made a good profit.

Having bought a house, they stripped it out, refurbished it with a septic tank, drainage, toilet, shower, new internal walls, kitchen and so on, and sold it on the British market.

The ethics of this may seem a bit 'dodgy'; that is, an estate agent buying and selling property is in a somewhat privileged position. In this instance, I didn't see a problem with it.

The owner was rich and wanted a sale. If I were to sell the house for £4,000, my commission would be about £100. It was hardly worth my while showing the place to a customer. If I bought it is as a *Marchand de Biens*, the owner would have his sale and I would probably make eight or nine thousand pounds after expenses. Someone stood to get a damned good deal. It might as well be me for once. God knew what I would do with the five acres of orchard and fields.

I immediately saw myself as a property tycoon, marching my way to riches.

"Bernard, my friend, I think that this is a very interesting property. But now I must leave. I have a train to catch."

"So, Alain, you're going to Paris. What is it, a woman?"

"Unfortunately not, Bernard."

"And then?"

"Oh well." I replied vaguely. "Just a bit of sight-seeing. It's quite exciting though."

His grunt deflated me. I sensed that he was not enamoured of the capital, or its people. "Don't know why you bother. Do you know Paris?"

"Yes, a bit. I went there a couple of times to sharpen up my French when I was studying for an exam."

"What do you think of it?"

I sought for that part of my opinion which I knew he would want to hear: "I can't say that I was very impressed with the civility of the Parisians, unlike the Bretons and Normans, who are almost always very polite." (This was true) "I know that they fancy themselves something rotten, always dreaming up fancy titles for themselves - 'The City of Light', 'Cultural Capital of Europe' and such like; and they seem to have a low opinion of the country people."

This had the desired affect.

"Pompous asses." He grumbled contemptuously, rubbing his unshaved chin. "Parasites who live on the country. I can tell you Monsieur, if they despise us, we don't have much time for them."

It was an opinion that I had heard more than once before. The capital/rest of the country divide is not a great one in England, but in France the town/country divide is real.

"What is a city, Monsieur, but a collection of parasites on the producers of food?"

I suppose if I'd known more about Parisian worthies, I could have parried along the lines of 'what have the Romans ever done for us?' by mentioning Pasteur, Madame Curie, Victor Hugho and so on, but to be honest, I didn't know which ones came from Paris.

"They serve up rubbish which they call Nouvelle Cuisine, the wooden-heads create fashions which almost make the mannequins blush, they live in noxious pollution at densities which would put a battery hen to shame, they drive like fools, they honk and swear at each other and live in perpetual tension and misery - when you arrive, be careful to regard closely the faces on the Métro, Alain - and the crime! Here I can leave my keys in my car, my house unlocked - there gangs fight in the street, marking out their territories with graffiti like dogs pissing against trees, pupils fight at knife point in the schools." He paused to fortify himself for another harangue.

"I saw it on the news last night. In Seine St Denis (North East Paris), robberies with violence are running at twenty a day sir! These people live like pigs on their own turf and when they come on holiday they lord it over us as if 1789 never happened!" He paused, as if searching for some other example of Parisian iniquity. It didn't take him long to find one. "My sister runs a guesthouse and loves to see you English; you are unassuming, you are polite, you rarely complain - even when you should - but the Parisians! They flock into the country in August and their arrogance and insolence are beyond belief!"

I was beginning to see that Bernard would be very happy to see the owner of the small house that we were standing in knocked down to half his asking price. Was this envy?

"Well, Bernard, I'm sure that you're right. At any rate, we'd better be getting on."

He grunted. "And I wish you the greatest of luck in your visit to our capital."

I parked-up at the station in Villedieu and took the train. The journey was to be about three hours and at first the carriages were fairly empty.

I wasn't going to Paris to see the sights. I was on my way for an interview. The job with Reg was not going as he had promised. My contract had not been raised. And, badger as I might, no attempt had been made to find me an office. It was hard for me to believe that I had found two dud jobs in a row, but it was beginning to look that way. Time would tell.

In the meantime, I had decided that it would be wise to look around for alternative employment and had contacted a couple of Parisian employment agencies. Today, I was meeting a prospective employer for a contract in my old profession, computing.

I settled down in my seat to go through all the points that the interviewer might cover. The train chugged its way east. Vire, Flers, Argente, L'Aigle (what a wonderful name, what can its origins have been?), Dreux, Versailles. I got off the train at the Parisian station of Montparnasse.

My final destination was La Défense, on the western edge of the city, about five miles from Montparnasse. I don't like underground trains. I find them dehumanising and faintly hostile, so I had no intention of following Bernard's advice and looking at the faces on the Métro.

Instead, I intended to have a brisk march across the city. Paris is a good city to walk in and I had planned what promised to be a very fine urban walk. From Montparnasse to the military college, then through the park down to the Eiffel Tower, across the Seine to the Palais de Chaillot, up to the Arc de Triomphe and down the Avenue de la Grande Armée (Napoleon's of course) and out to La Défense.

Paris! Seeing the vast concourse of one of the world's greatest cities, it's marvels and follies, great buildings, gardens, shops, churches, cafés, beggars and pretty girls.

I am tall and have long legs, so my natural pace is fast. In a city it is perhaps four miles per hour. My feet hit the pavement in a rhythm which eats up the distance. Heart beating. Oxygen flowing. Blood coursing. Alert, alive, cruising past people, changing gear. Such walking is a kind of hypnosis and good for the spirit. Only once do I remember going out on a city walk in a foul mood and coming back in the same foul mood. My walk would prepare me for my interview as no end of study would.

Such was the theory. But if Bernard had already put a bit of a damper on my trip, the weather was to do the same for my walking plans. Damper and damper and damper. It was raining. Pouring. Bucketing. Teeming. Lashing. So I took the Métro.

Rather than study the faces of my fellow commuters for traces of fear, or tension, or anger, as Bernard had suggested, I settled down to ponder on what I was going through. This was not a metaphysical observation of my life and its tribulations. It was more of a geological one concerning the underside of Paris itself. On what lay above, below and alongside me.

144

If you were to see a model of the undersides of Paris, the Métro would be just a layer of pipes in a warren of other excavations. Above them lie the sewers. Victor Hugo devotes a whole chapter of the masterpiece which he wrote in Jersey, *Les Miserables*, to the wanderings of Valjean through the sewers to escape from the law. To give you a taste of the complexity of those sewers, and indeed of the book:

"Valjean started by making a mistake, He thought he was under the Rue Saint-Denis and it was unfortunate that he was not. There is an old stone sewer dating from Louis XIII under the Rue Saint-Denis, having only a single turn, under the former Cour des Miracles, and a single branch, the Saint-Martin sewer, of which the four arms intersect. But the Petite-Truanderie passage, of which the entrance is near the Corinth tavern, has never communicated with that under the Rue-St-Denis; it runs into the Montmarte sewer and this was the way Valjean had followed.

Here there are endless chances of going astray, the Montmarte sewer being one of the most labyrinthine of all. Fortunately he had left behind him the Les Halles sewer, the plan of which is like a forest of ships' masts; but more than one perplexity lay ahead of him, more than one street corner (for streets are what they really are) offered itself in the darkness like a question mark. First, on his left, the huge Platrière sewer, a sort of Chinese puzzle, running with countless twists and turns under the Hotel des Postes and the corn market to the Seine; secondly, on his right, the Rue de Cadran with its

three blind alleys; thirdly, again on the left, a sort of
fork zig-zagging into the basin of the Louvre; and
finally, on the right, the blind alley of the Rue des
Jeuneurs, without counting small offshoots here
and there - all this before he reached the ring sewer,
which alone could take him to some place sufficiently
far to be safe.

Had Valjean known all this he would have realised,
simply by feeling the wall, that he could not be under
the Rue Saint-Denis...."

Of course he would, silly boy. He simply wasn't paying
attention. Perhaps he should have taken the book. Alice
swears that you could find your way underground from one
side of the city to the other just by reading it.

And didn't *The Hunchback of Notre Dame* (another of
Hugo's) spend his time scrabbling about under the cathedral
when he wasn't ringing the bells? Come to think of it, doesn't
the same go for *The Phantom of the Opera*? Also, Cartouche,
the legendary Parisian bandit, was often underground, popping
up here and there to carry out his daring depredations. They
might have all met up for soireés, those ringing, stabbing,
pinching boys - *qui peut dire*?

I don't know why Disney hasn't interested himself in this
possibility. It would be ideal for a cartoon:

Valjean (to hunchback); "Hey, hunchback. How ya' hangin'?"

Hunchback: "Hangin' is right amigo. Nothing but tollin' them
damn bells all day. It's doin' my head in."

Phantom (silkily): "That perhaps explains your lack of intellect
my friend. The bells have addled your brains."

Valjean. "Lay offen ma buddy, Phantom."

Cartouche (a Mexican bandit mouse with the requisite

sombrero). "Oh, caramba mes amigos. We donna have to fight among ourselves when the whole world is agen us. I have a leetle plan to separate Cardinal Richelieu from his jewels and geeve them to the poor. What say you, comrados?"

Valjean: "Eh man, gi me five. I'm in."

All sing: "Above our heads the rich folks play,
while in darkness we flee the day.
Misery our lot and fear and dirt,
for the wicked Richelieu doth wish us hurt."

Etc, etc.

But if they had met underground, they wouldn't have necessarily met in the sewers.

For the sewers, two thousand three hundred kilometres of them though there are, are only another thread in the skein of Paris under Paris.

There are deeper, more profound, larger, more mysterious and infinitely more dangerous gulfs and fissures, chasms and caverns under the city. They extend for more than three hundred kilometres and go under the whole of old Paris on both sides of the Seine making the sub-strata of the city akin to a gruyere cheese.

But where did they all come from, these strange vast spaces under the modern city streets? To put it simply, (and it is quite simple really), the buildings of Paris were constructed from the rock upon which they stand and the holes this left are, not surprisingly, still there.

Most of those holes have been there a very long time, the oldest being Roman. When the Romans arrived in Gaul, they took limestone, gypsum and clay from the soil for their buildings. Even then, there were catacombs. They built their arena on top of an old quarry.

Like the Romans, all succeeding generations continued to quarry for limestone, gypsum and clay.

From the twelfth century onwards, vast building works meant more and deeper quarrying. There just wasn't enough limestone left on the surface to build the Chatelet Palaces, churches, abbeys, the Louvre and the town walls, so they went under the city. The miners were 'only those who were capable of accepting trying and dangerous conditions', often from poor regions or ex-criminals. Sometimes they dug deep vertical shafts and then struck out horizontally from the shaft bottom, driving tunnels in all directions. These, of course, frequently met up with other tunnels and shafts. Sometimes, as at the Luxembourg quarries on the Left (south) Bank, they dug a gentle slope so that they could get wagons and horses in.

From the start of the fifteenth century, a new technique of infilling the limestone-denuded caverns was developed, using the mass of stone left over from the quarrying (about seventy-five percent) to fill in the spaces. The loose stone was buttressed with dry-stone walls. This method allowed stone to be removed from beneath entire quarters of the city, while the streets did not collapse (well, not at the time at least).

In the gypsum quarries (gypsum is used to make plaster), the rock was less stable, the supporting pillars closer together and the roof higher, up to sixty feet high. Strangely enough, the fire of London in 1666 gave plaster a big boost. Because it was seen that plaster-coated walls had withstood the fire much better than wooden ones, King Louis XIV ordered that all French building timber should henceforward be plastered over to retard fire. Of course he insisted on Plaster of Paris. This alone caused sixty-five hectares of new quarries to be excavated. Such was the demand for gypsum that these were often three stories deep.

Limestone and gypsum were even exported to America. It was only in 1813 that new quarries were banned and quarrying itself didn't end until 1910.

Then there is clay. The clay was used for pottery, bricks and tiles. Even in Roman times the quarries were up to a hundred feet deep. It is known that there are 835 hectares of abandoned limestone quarries and 2350 hectares (about nine square miles) of gypsum mines under the capital. For clay we can only guess. Being plastic, the shafts have a habit of closing up on themselves because of the huge weight of the buildings above them.

The clay was often found under the limestone, so frequently there are levels of mine upon mine. Being only about four feet high, these clay workings were incredibly punishing to work in, the men crouching, crawling, even lying down, often in mud, with bellows giving what little air they could from above, getting hotter and hotter, with always the danger of hitting trapped water in the clay. According to a contemporary account: 'They have the choice of three types of death; being asphyxiated, drowned or crushed.'

For many centuries, the ancient shafts were simply built over and ignored. Deserted and untended, they were prone to pressure from above, land settlement and water seepage. Only at the end of the eighteenth century did dramatic street and building collapses remind the Parisians of the true nature of what was under their feet.

The quarries have seen many uses. Smugglers and thieves have used them to stash their loot and during the war they were used by both Germans and Resistants alike. Some are still used as wine cellars. Others are vast bone stores. This is the case under all of the cemeteries in central Paris. When there are too many bodies (in times of war, famine or disease), the bodies are simply 'put downstairs'. Under the cemetery of Montparnasse, for example, there is a pattern of streets, at the centre of which stands 'The Crossroads of Death'. It lies directly under the same crossroads on the surface.

The official 'Catacombs of Paris' at Denfert-Rochereau are open to the public. But they cover only a minute part of all the galleries which flow under the French capital.

Most of the network is closed to the public, visited only by the teams employed by the city to patrol the galleries and tunnels, rebuilding walls and pillars and neatly stacking up the bones. Sometimes, as the walls warp and shift, new discoveries are made. For example in 1990 an inspector discovered a previously unknown coal mine down there.

Actually, that's not quite the whole story. With a network so huge, there have obviously in times past been many hundreds of entrances. Officialdom has stopped up most of these; but they are constantly being broken into or new ones made. There is even a special police force to stop illegal entry.

There are some people who are addicted to descending into the strange caverns and grottoes and finding the underground lakes and statues (there have been some surprisingly artistic people down there). Maps of the entrances are published, some on the internet (where there are also photographs). There are currently up to a hundred or more people 'visiting' (quite illegally) these wildernesses at night, mostly during the week-end. I hope for their sakes they keep clear of the clay cuts.

A tannoy breaks into my reverie.

"*La Défense.*" Oh, wake up Biggins! *Nous sommes arrivées*, as they say round here.

A glance out of the Métro revealed that it was still raining in all those extravagant ways that it had been earlier. Now it was raining cats and dogs as well. This was bad news. I don't know why - although crass stupidity has to be a main contender - I had no raincoat with me. Nor was I sure exactly how to get to my destination. In these circumstances, it is always the case that there is nobody around. Consequently, I went up to the top of the steps and out on to a vast expanse of pavement. I was in the highrise quarter of La Défense, built to the west of Paris and away from the historic centre so as not to destroy the harmony of scale of the rest of the city. Clever really,

Someone might have suggested something along those lines to the Planning Department of the City of London after the Second World War, (if the City of London had a planning department after the Second World War, perhaps it was bombed. The most feasible alternative, that some poor guy was given a short initiation which consisted of teaching him to say the words: 'I don't need to see the plans, put the crap up where you like. You'll find the rubber stamp on the desk. Leave the money in the normal place', is too horrible to contemplate.)

I ran across the thousand acre pedestrian concourse towards the tower block, La Défense itself. La Défense is like the small letter 'n' with square corners multiplied several million fold. It must be a couple of hundred feet tall. It has offices up both sides of the 'n' and, this is the incredible bit, *across the top as well.* How these are supported is anyone's guess, but I'm not sure I'd like to work in them.

Scurrying across the concourse, I felt like a fly on a table, with a giant throwing jugs of water at me. By the time that I had got into the tower block, I was soaked to the skin.

Needless to say, I was in the wrong office block. By the time

I had run the mile to the other side of the concourse, I was not only soaked to the skin, my shoes were threatening to disintegrate.

Given this somewhat discouraging start, the interview went very well. Monsieur Simon asked some searching questions. Had I worked with such-and-such a software package? Yes I had. Had I used such-and-such a computer? Yes I had. Could I answer some questions about it? Yes I could, and did.

From there on in, I warmed up and became more forthcoming. The contract sounded a very interesting one. Project managing the technical side of the installation of a new system across five countries. Most of my time would be split between England and France.

It was essential that I speak French, as the software was a replacement for a package already in use in France. There was a suspicion locally that it was all an Anglo-American plan to do-down the honest French folk.

By the time the interview was over, Monsieur Simon had asked me when I could start and introduced me to some colleagues. All good signs. His parting words were: "I'll just have to get sign-off from the Financial Director. I'll let your agency know tomorrow."

After a time as a computer contractor, you get to the point where little surprises you. Jobs which are 'desperately urgent' turn out to start in three months time (or never), 'routine interviews' can turn out to be like grillings by the SS. 'In-depth tests' can end up being informal chats. I knew when I left La Défense that I had won Mr Simon over. I also strongly suspected that he would have serious problems winning over his Financial Director. I was right on both counts.

I went home and sent a fax to Reg outlining *the Marchand de Biens* property. In it, I repeated my - by now routine - queries about my office and contract.

A week later, I was told that the Parisian project had been put on 'indefinite hold'.

Oh well, there was still the *Marchand de Biens*.

SELLING FRENCH DREAMS

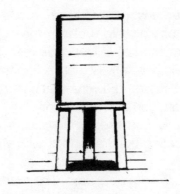

The magic of France. Preparing the course.
From the horse's mouth. Time for a practical.

"Every man has two countries; his own and France."

I can't remember who said that, but surprisingly, I don't think he was French. Perhaps it's not so surprising. To the inhabitant of the British Isles, France has an awful lot of attractions. Our own thoughts about it were probably typical of those of the hundreds of people I've talked with.

Picture a day in late summer. It is hot and drowsy. The heat is almost sultry. Something tells you that behind it all lies rain; that before the day is out, the sky will rumble like a flexed tin sheet; then rip apart to let down a deluge which will wash all the dust from the air and leave the mysterious night cleansed and alive with the chirping of crickets and the hooting of owls and night jars. If you were to walk down to the village then, you'd do it in the company of the infinite, under a great starlit sky.

Your holiday has brought you to an idyllic spot. Forgotten, for the moment, the traffic, the fumes, the noise, the hustle and bustle of British life. There isn't another house in view.

You've just had a wonderful lunch, made up from half a dozen bowls of stuff which you got from the supermarché and fresh stuff from the market. Olives. Potatoes. Beetroot. Fish. Cheese. Paté. Quiche. With it went a baguette (they never taste as good in Britain), red wine that costs a quid or two a bottle. To finish off, you had a flan from the bakery. A great huge apple flan, with sour cream. Now you're onto the coffee and a tot; and feeling quite at peace with yourself and the world.

Peace. That's the keynote here. The roads are quiet, the villages are quiet. There's little to disturb except the cockerel and the crickets. And it's warm. So warm. You can feel the warmth seeping into your body; it's as if it's thawing a part of you that's been frozen for a whole northern year.

What better to do now than have forty winks? There's nothing demanding to be done (except the washing up; and that'll have to wait). There never seems to be anything here that won't wait a while. It's all so laid back.

Down in the village, you'd swear the place hasn't changed for fifty years. The paint's peeling a bit on the houses. The *Mairie* in the square has a bike leaning against it which owes everything to the black delivery breed and nothing to the Tour de France. The church stands timeless above the churchyard, with it's brownstone tower and its half open shutter just below the spire. On the hour, its single bell tolls. But only once.

Slow, peaceful, polite, friendly, clean. There's no grafitti here; and the locals nod and say good day to you as if you'd lived here all your life.

And the space! The outbuildings lie empty, except for the

barbecue and the deckchairs and the pile of wood. They seem to go on forever. The garden does too. When you think what a place like this would fetch at home - if a place like this existed at home - you feel like a millionaire. And round here you almost are. Why, you could sell up your very ordinary house in Britain and buy half the village! With a few chickens, free wood, cheap booze and the orchard, you'd be halfway there. Think what your friends would say! They'd be pea-green with envy! One flew over the cuckoo's nest.

It's all true though! It could work! You could do-up the outbuildings, turn them into *gites* or bed and breakfast and make a living. Why, look at the number of people who go on holiday to France; and how difficult it always is to get hold of a place; sometimes you need to book a year ahead!

And so you dream the very same dream that a million other British visitors a year are dreaming. And like them, you go home, think of more practical things and forget it for another year. Or do you....

Maybe you're one of the more adventurous spirits, someone with a bit of pluck, a bit of get up and go, a deeper yearning. Whatever your reason, perhaps you're one of those who progress to stage two; the French property show.

There are a number of these which do the rounds and they're very popular. Visitors fall into two categories, those who are looking for a holiday home and those who are looking to move to France permanently. The former generally get a good deal when they buy; a property in France for a fraction of the price that they would pay in Britain. A property which is full of character and which, if they've chosen wisely, will give them - and probably their family and friends - a good deal of pleasure.

The latter often get a great deal more than they bargained

for. The fact is that for a great many of those who move to France, the dream will go wrong and they will be leaving again - or trying to - pretty quickly. The cost to them is usually high.

How many is 'a great many'? It's hard to be precise, but in 'our' bit of Normandy, Dick reckoned that half the people who moved there would be on their way back, or trying to go back, within two years. From my own observations and investigations, I would think that he was probably right. Reg put it slightly lower for Northern Brittany; perhaps a third. Maybe it varies from region to region, I don't know. It's certainly not a secret. While I was preparing the course, I was approached by a French student at Caen university who was doing a thesis on the subject.

The figures don't seem to improve with time, either. A television programme that I saw on those buying farms in France - obviously a fairly committed breed - also spoke of half moving back to Britain. That was in 2001, while I was writing this book.

And the cost? As I've said before, the buyer pays about a twenty percent overhead in taxes and charges, which he is unlikely to recoup on selling. Worse, he may have difficulty selling at all. It's very much a buyer's market in much of rural France.

But money is only part of the cost. A fellow author on France, and resident, George East, who is as saddened as I by this cataclysmic waste, made the point very movingly in his book *René and Me* (La Puce Publications, 1997):

> "Graham's business has failed, the debts have
> mounted and he is now living elsewhere. It is a
> familiar but always tragic story, and one which
> haunts us every day ...To see all those days,

weeks and years of effort and expense wasted is a truly depressing experience for us. How the thousands who put all their hope and money into the fabric of an eventually ruined dream must feel is hardly conceivable, and an experience we must not allow ourselves to endure."

My knowledge has its limits (has a full study ever been made?) But I am quite certain - and I hope that I have quoted enough first and second hand evidence to explain why - that for an appallingly high proportion of those who move to France, that move ends in tears. Why? Sometimes the problem lies with the dreamers themselves. I've written elsewhere about the couple - he was a butcher - and their children whom I took around some houses and then, at his request, around an abbatoir looking for work for the father.

With little money, young children, looking to buy in an isolated area, they quite simply had not the slightest idea what they were letting themselves in for; and not the slightest chance of success. I hope they believed me when I told them that was the case.

The butcher from Birmingham was an extreme but by no means unique case of lack of research. Rosy-glow dreams of rural France blind some people just as readily as smart uniforms, flashy business prospectuses, Dutch tulip bulbs or internet shares blind others.

But lack of basic preparation, or common sense, is by no means the only reason why so many of those who move to France will find that they have made an expensive mistake. Nor, indeed, is it the most common one. There are lots of reefs to avoid. Now that I had finished preparing my course on living in France, I had found thirteen of them; and by no means all were obvious. (Thirteen may seem a rather contrived number, but I have not made the figure up. I have listed them in the appendix at the end of this book.)

It had been hard work preparing the course, even though I had help with it. Perhaps my most important helper was Peter Edwards, an Englishman who worked for another immobilier, speaks fluent French and had lived in France for years. He had seen many Britons come and go and had lots of experience with setting up businessess. He had a deep knowledge of the legal aspects of buying property, an area in which my own knowledge was poor. In short, he was an all-round expert.

Peter shared my view that while it is fine to 'simply sell the dream' of France to those who are buying holiday homes, we were not happy to do so to people like the Birmingham butcher.

(While I think that it is greatly to the credit of any agent who takes this approach, I can sympathise with those who do not. In putting-off anyone who is dreaming as deeply as my butcher friend, the agent will undoubtedly save his customer from a very rude awakening. He will, however, do it at his own expense, for he will have spent time and money talking himself out of a sale. While probably most agents would show such humanity, self-sacrifice and risk - for it can be dangerous to waken a dreamer too quickly - others take the approach that their job is simply to sell houses, not to be a free advice centre.)

Peter himself had been producing similar material to the stuff I was writing (as I'm sure have many other diligent agents, across the length and breadth of France). Unlike me, he was not in the age of the computer, so could not produce it professionally.

When I showed him my work and suggested that there

were areas where he might not have any experience, Peter, by no means an arrogant man, said that he doubted it. As we worked our way through the course notes, I realised that he was right. He <u>had</u> seen it all before. With his help I completed my preparation. My course material ran, as I mentioned earlier, to over a hundred pages.

Apart from using Peter to help with the more complicated questions about doing business, I was lucky enough to have the help of another friend, Mike, an Englishman who lived near by, and who is a structural engineer and surveyor.

As well as the expertise they brought, there were two other reasons why I wanted to use Peter and Mike. Having three presenters would save my audience from the boredom of listening to me drone on interminably. And they both offered me their help for nothing; an important consideration for a new and risky venture.

I had grouped my material into subject areas, buying property, health, education, and so on. Now I timed how long it would take to deliver to my audience, taking into account meal breaks and making it as interesting as possible by getting the audience involved. I found that, at a push, it could be done in two days - thus making a weekend course possible.

Then I found a venue. I had considered holding the course in England. That would have been more convenient for my customers. However, as I thought a visit to some properties would be invaluable, I finally decided to hold it in France. The course was to be residential. As it would be important to look at peoples' circumstances and needs very specifically, I had decided to restrict the first course to eight people.

Having been to see quite a few possible venues, I chose an 'establishment' near the sea, run by an English lady called Pat.

Pat was an artist who had made a fine, dignified, Norman house into a very comfortable 'B & B'. The rooms were airy and clean. There were lots of rugs and stripped wood, and paintings and flowers everywhere. The place was very restful and welcoming. What was more, she was an excellent cook. Pat spoke good French and had found friends in her area; she was very definitely someone who had 'made it' in France.

Then I explained what I was doing to the editors of the English magazines devoted to France. They were aware of the problem and sympathetic. I was encouraged by their response, which included editorial coverage. I advertised in two of them and waited with bated breath.

The replies came in. I had bookings from four couples. I had filled my first course.

The morning of my customers' arrival found me preparing the room and in a fairly jittery state. Standing up to talk to a room full of strangers is bad enough. When they are paying you and you are 'The Expert' delivering your own material for the first time, it is ten times worse. Nervously I set up my whiteboard, checked that the marker pens worked, and put pads, paper and notes around the table. I checked that there was water and biscuits and finalised the time of the coffee break.

What if they bowled questions that I could not answer? What if they found the presentation boring, or irrelevant? Could I justify their long journey, travelling expenses and course cost? What about mannerisms? I'd read somewhere that you should never jingle the change in your pocket. The clock seemed to take forever to advance a single minute....

At last they arrived. I welcomed them, asked them how their

trip over had been, introduced myself and got them to talk a little about themselves. The couples ranged in age from their mid-thirties to their mid-sixties. Two couples intended to retire and the other two to work. They were all from southern England. Then I gave them a brief outline of what the course was about. It was to help them. As they were planning to move abroad, they were playing for very high stakes indeed.....

The British Medical Council publishes a table which allows you to measure the amount of stress you have suffered during the last year. It lists various events, such as moving house, changing a job and so on. These are given points.

You tot up the points to see whether you are near the danger level. Above that line, your health and relationships are at risk. Moving a lifestyle, a culture and a country takes you right up to the line.

The way I picture it is that the voyage of the Briton moving to live in France is like that of a ship coming across the sea, weighed dangerously low by the load it is carrying. In front of that ship are a number of reefs, any one of which can wreck it. Far, far too many have gone aground on those reefs already. Each such accident is, to a greater or lesser degree, damaging to an individual or a family; but it is not inevitable. As the reefs are fixed, they can be avoided. Some are easy to see, some less so.

The three most commonly used ways of finding those reefs all have fairly serious drawbacks.

Literature on the subject, while being good on technical aspects such as the legal process, tends to ignore the subjects of learning French and integrating socially. Also, books don't answer when you ask them questions.

Relying on the estate agent is unfair to the agent and dangerous for the customer. The agent's opinions are certainly worth considering on some points, for example where to buy (town or country), and what to buy (ruin or sound house), but it would be totally unfair on that agent - and stupid of the customer - to ask him for advice on *whether* to buy. It would be silly, of course, to ask any salesman that question, but even sillier to ask the agent in France, who is typically paid only if he makes a sale, and in some cases pays for his own expenses.

I was stating the obvious here, but I was doing so because I had personally often been asked by customers for advice on the viability of their schemes; indeed that was one reason why I had created the course.

Finally, trial and error is a good way to find disaster; but a poor one to avoid it. In Bismarck's words: "Only a fool learns from his experiences. A wise man learns from the experiences of others." Which is where this course came in. It was largely based on my survey of others who had already made the dangerous crossing - over a hundred of them - and their experiences. To mix my metaphors a bit, where better to hear it than from the horse's mouth?

The aim of that survey, and my course, was to map *all* of the reefs. Mine was, as far as I knew, the fullest chart which had ever been drawn.

In other words, I was re-iterating the reasons my customers had come. We were on the same side!

Next, I talked about notaires and immobiliers and how much they charge. It's always a bit of a culture shock to the British that the buyer pays the costs of purchase and how much those costs are. Property prices have to rise substantially before those costs can be recouped.

Time for tea.

After tea, I handed over to Peter. There can be few things more calculated to change a normally sane, intelligent and receptive person into a glazed-over, mouth-frothing, twitching madman than 'Suspensive clauses in the *Compromis de Vente*' (sale agreement). They, along with knowing what legal entity to buy with, are two of those reefs which can destroy the move to France. (A letter to *France News* illustrates this brilliantly and - hard to believe - wittily. I have included it in the appendix).

Peter covered these points and a number of others,

Then it was time for lunch, to which I had invited a couple of other British residents, so that we could continue the discussion while we ate.

After lunch, I got Mike to speak about recurring costs and essential services. This covered rates, insurance, water, drainage, and electricity. The reader may have noticed that the French electricity system is, from bitter experience, something that I'm a bit of an expert on. Which is precisely why I didn't want to talk about it. If I start on that subject, I can - and will - bore for hours. I just can't help myself. He also talked about gas, wood, telephones and television and radio.

I'm a radio man myself, but one of the recommendations to come out of my survey was to 'try to receive British television'. In practice most Britons who can pick up British T.V. do so. When changing so much, language, culture, life style, etc, it's helpful to try and hang onto something. Unless, of course, you don't like television; or you wish to say 'I renounce Britain and all it stands for!' (In itself a dangerous sentiment. Disillusion with one's own country is not always a sound basis for living in another).

Time for tea.

The day was going well and provoking a lot of questions and discussions. For the last session, I tackled moving and everyday life. There are two reefs here; the *Carte de Sejour* and health insurance. To (legally) live full-time in France, one needs a *Carte de Sejour*, or residency permit. To get it, you must prove that you can support yourself financially. (I don't know how the French authorities manage to reconcile this with the fact that we Europeans are all supposed to be integrated now, but it is the law).

We spoke about health for quite a long time, as it is a complicated subject.

As none of those on the course intended to bring children, I did not discuss another reef - education. But, of course, for those with kids (like us!), it's an absolutely crucial part of *la vie Francaise*. One of the survey recommendations had been 'don't put your children into French schools after the age of seven'.

This was not a unanimous recommendation (some had managed it). Personally, I would agree with it. Successful integration into the education system gets very much harder after the age of seven; partly because the all-important grammar begins to be taught from that age.

Common wisdom that 'kids adapt quickly - they'll be talking like a native in three months' is, in my experience, nonsense. Our kids took about twelve months - and they're both bright and I speak French. Language is not only learned at school, but at home. If the parent cannot help with homework, or correct mistakes, the learning process will be slowed down. And of course the move is stressful for the child - taken away from his or her friends and put into a situation where s/ he can not speak the language has a very serious affect on some children.

In short: To be a success for the family, the move must be a success for every member of it. For the children this becomes less and less likely after the age of seven or eight.

At last, in the early evening, the first day came to a close and we sat down to dinner together. I was greatly relieved to hear that the comments were very positive. I drove home in a happy mood. After all my time, effort and worry, at last I knew for sure that my course was worthwhile - and that it worked!

We spent the first part of the second day discussing making a living in France. Considering that two of our couples were retired, I had expected them to duck out of this. However, both were keen to carry on. The group was beginning to feel like an extended family now.

I gave this part of the course. Business planning is a subject that interests me, and having worked as a business analyst for a good few years, one that I know a bit about. Not surprisingly, the greatest number (four) of those dangerous reefs that can sink the unwary are to do with doing business. The first of these is financial planning; and one of the survey recommendation was 'Don't be too ambitious in business plans'.

In general, the ratio of British business failures to successes in France is high. There are many reasons. Some failures are caused by over-optimistic projections of earnings, some by not being pessimistic enough about costs. Either is potentially fatal. Then there is timing. Getting a business off the ground can be a slow process, especially in a foreign country.

Another reef is the legality of the work.

If a house is to be used as a business, or if you are working from home, this may have to be stipulated when the property is purchased (back to suspensive clauses in the *Compromis de Vente!*).

Working for someone else has its pitfalls too. A third of the people I spoke to for my survey said: 'Be wary of people'. Part of this is to do with employers; are they honest, competent, and, perhaps more importantly, operating legally. (Obviously, if you are working for France Telecom this is unlikely to be a problem.) This is an obscure reef, but one of the most difficult to avoid.

A stranger in a foreign land is peculiarly vulnerable. He will be unaware of the reputations of those with whom he is dealing, which makes him a natural target for the unscrupulous. As the Allies knew during the war, you are most vulnerable to attack at the moment of landing.

The surest defence is the contract. This should cover all the verbally agreed conditions, and it should be signed by both parties BEFORE being used as a justification for moving.

'Gentlemen's agreements' are particularly to be avoided. I've no idea why gentlemen should be averse to committing their promises to paper. Indeed, it seems to me that the exact opposite should be the case.....

A break for tea.

After tea, we discussed two more of the reefs for those doing business; sales and marketing. A market must exist for the service, and the service must be succesfully sold. In my experience, the world does not beat a path to your door whether you build a better mousetrap or not. It only does so in response to advertising (and later, if you offer a good enough service, by recommendation).

Both the working couples on my course were planning to offer bed and breakfast accommodation. So we considered the different ways of getting custom; going it alone or as part of a group. We also talked about the length of the letting season. The landlady, Pat, joined us for this and was very helpful.

I summed up this part of the course with my analogy of a chain. With business, too, it's of no value having one superb link (normally the product), if the others will not hold. Every link is vital! No link must fail!

Time for lunch. Mike joined us. He was to be our mentor for the first afternoon session, a 'practical', for we were to leave the classroom and see some real houses....

We visited two properties. The first was an old water mill about ten miles from Avranches. The place had been superbly modernised, keeping its character; so that the living room looked down on the old mill wheel. A French window gave out onto the garden through which the stream flowed. It was a stunningly attractive property in the middle of nowhere. Here we talked about what to think of *before* looking at houses.

After crowded Britain, many people tend to favour rural properties with fields for miles around - like the mill. This is very often a mistake. As well as meaning that one has to drive everywhere, it leads to problems in socialising. If you are constantly in reach of and see people, you are much more likely to integrate than if you are the unknown foreigner who lives in a house down the end of a lane at the other end of the

Commune.

Of course, for anyone thinking of offering Bed and Breakfast, it is counter-productive to be hidden down a farm track miles away from anywhere. It is better to be on (or near and sign-posted from) a main road. This may sound astoundingly simple advice, but there are those who never think of it, simply expecting that all their trade will come from pre-booking. This severely limits their potential custom, sometimes fatally so.

Then we went to the other extreme, a tumbledown house in the middle of a field with access along a rough track. This was to illustrate another reef: the cost of renovation. Many people wildly underestimate these costs and simply run out of money (or end up living in a semi-ruin). Mike took us round the place, explaining what to look for in the structure of a house and giving an idea of what the various renovations would cost. Surveys are not automatic on French houses. Indeed they are rare.

And, as Mike explained, it's not just the work which needs doing - it's who you get to do it. He re-iterated a point that I had made that morning; the newcomer is vulnerable.

British builders in France vary, like every other group in the world, from the superb to the appalling. As I've said earlier, it was because of this that Dick had compiled his list of good workmen; and his blacklist. And there are some very bad builders. I could write a chapter of horrifying tales. French builders aren't all saints either. The temptation to rook the rich *étranger* is not always ignored. The best way to find a builder is by recommendation; and a good artisan will be happy to supply references. The key point is to be suspicious.

Mike hammered out the basic rules of estimating for, and carrying out, renovations. Again, they mostly seemed obvious.

Again, they are frequently ignored. (I have listed these in the appendix).

Mike was superb. A thoroughly practical man.

Then we returned to the Bed and Breakfast for the last part of my course. This was about the social considerations of living in rural France, where lie the last two reefs: learning the language and making friends. These are every bit as important as the practical considerations. They are the make or break of the move. Too often they are the break.

I think that the reason why these subjects are so often under-estimated or ignored by books on France, is because there are a lot of cosy assumptions about them that you only realise are wrong if you've actually lived in the country. In other words, I think the only way to get to the nitty-gritty was to carry out a survey of the British who live there, as I had.

'Learn the language!' was the second most popular recommendation from my survey. This may be blindingly obvious; but there are a number of misconceptions which cloud the issue. For example, the popular sentiment 'everyone speaks English anyway' is balderdash.

In thirty or fifty years, France may have caught up in the world language stakes; but they're not there yet. For instance, of perhaps thirty notaires and their clerks whom I know, only one speaks English. Doctors are the second most likely to speak English (after teachers), but the percentage is still quite small; and I don't know a single French mechanic, electrician, plumber or builder who does.

Nor are the officials who deal with tax, insurance, driving documents and so-on likely to speak English. Not surprisingly, the few British residents who are bi-lingual don't want to spend their time on the routine communications of those who are not.

It is difficult to get by without a reasonable grasp of French.

Another glib conception is 'It'll be easy to pick up French when I get there.' It's perfectly true that the best way to learn a language is by total immersion. Unfortunately you're unlikely to get total immersion unless your French is already good (and the non-swimmer who is totally immersed is more likely to drown than to learn to swim). This is a catch twenty-two situation which my survey had picked up quite clearly.

In the survey I asked the question "How good was your French when you arrived and how good is it now?" The possible responses were, 'non-existent', 'poor', 'reasonable', 'good', 'fluent' and 'bi-lingual' (fluent being good enough to handle telephone calls). Only where the person concerned was employed by a French firm, or dealt closely with French people, had their level of French improved by more than one notch; often they didn't think that it had improved at all.

None of this is helped by jolly books which claim that you can learn French in three months, ten days, overnight or by hypnosis. If that were true, what would be the point of GCSEs, 'A' levels and degrees? The chief aim of these exams is to train people to speak, read and write French and they take years of study.

Most people with 'A' level French do not claim to be able to speak the language, and it takes seven years (part-time) study to get that far. Personally, it took me years of constant practice and grammatical exercises before I became at all fluent in French, and I don't think that I'm the exception.

Another misconception is that you only need a small vocabulary. For shopping this may be true. To integrate into the community and form friendships, it is not. The third most popular recommendation from the survey was 'Make friends with the French.' It was noticeable that those who said this had, without exception, a level of French which they classed as 'good' or higher; and that the levels of stress they had experienced (another question in the survey) were lower than those with poorer French.

An attitude common to Britons moving to France is that they do not want to mix with other Britons, but want to integrate with the French. It is noticeable that in the majority of cases this attitude changes as people recognise the importance of having some social contact with their fellow countrymen.

Cutting off your roots in the hope of growing better ones is in itself a high risk strategy. If the new roots don't grow, it can lead to loneliness and disillusion. And, for the expatriate, new roots - friendships - often grow very slowly, and only at the cost of very hard work.

Friendships are based on having something in common; such as a sense of humour, interests or background. Many cultural references are to T.V. or radio.

For example, I'm sure I could spin out a comfortable hour with a perfect stranger of my generation recreating the lost Sunday world of the early 1960's, Jimmy Clitheroe and World Wide Family Favourites on the wireless, with Jean Metcalf from Cologne -

"This is from 23456127, Sgt Brown of BFPO 42
to his wife Emily and their children Tony and
Susan of Dernworth, near Bristol. Wishing you
all my love and see you at Christmas. He'd like us
to play Tommy Steele's 'Little white bull.''

Then we could get nostalgic about tea - which always consisted of salmon with white sliced bread and butter followed by tinned fruit - in the front room that we only used once a week.

I don't know how I would do that in French.

Apart from that, it is, of course, much more difficult for people speaking different languages to become friends. So much time and effort is spent actually communicating, and it is so mentally draining, that the 'pay-off' - the enjoyment of talking - can get lost. This can easily lead either party to become discouraged and see the exchange as a chore, so that they become reluctant to go through the exercise again.

Those who had most successfully integrated said: 'Make an effort. Making friends will be hard work and it will be you, the newcomer, who will have to make the running!'

It's not all doom and gloom however. The survey also showed that there are certain people who seem to find adjusting to a different culture much easier than others. These are artists, musicians and those who are used to living abroad, for example servicemen and women.

I wrapped-up the course by reviewing what we had already discussed. Then I did a 'count down' of the recommendations which had come from my survey, the most popular of which was 'try before you buy.' That is, to take a long- term rental before buying. All but one of the hundred and six people whom I questioned recommended renting, for periods of between six and twenty-four months.

The advantages renting gives are many. It gives the prospective buyer the opportunity to get to know an area, and choose the best place to live, at leisure. More importantly, perhaps, renting gives him, or her, the chance to test whether the move lives up to expectations before spending a lot of money and burning bridges. On a more personal note, someone whose stated intent is to *try* living abroad looks far less of a fool if the trial is not successful. These advantages (and there are others as well), generally far outweigh the disadvantages.

Rental properties are often available from estate agents. If they are British, they should be sympathetic to 'try before you buy', after all, they have probably snagged on a reef or two themselves. Three of the respondents in my survey were British agents. All three recommended renting first.

Finally we wound-down with a social evening of good food, wine and chat. The course had been hard work but enjoyable. I was very pleased with the comments which my customers made on the questionnaire that I had given them. I think that they were equally pleased with the course.

As I mentioned earlier, I have listed the recommendations and 'reefs' in the appendix. I was soon to be given personal proof of the accuracy of my chart; for I was shortly to be driven squarely onto one of those reefs myself. One that would rip the bottom from our own flimsy craft, and leave us struggling in deep water.....

SELLING FRENCH DREAMS

Books. The thirteenth reef. My exam.

It was a phone call which sparked off the chain of events that ended my time as an estate agent. The call came from a notaire with whom I had worked in the past and with whom I had stayed in contact. He was (and is) a very interesting and intelligent man who had always been a good friend to me. Recently he had warned me that the authorities were looking 'very closely' at British agents in Normandy. Today his message was blunt. I must read that day's local newspaper, the *Manche Libre*. Urgently. At once. Now.

But I will come back to that momentous call later. Let me start on a bright note. Fine things were happening with my book, *A Normandy Tapestry*.

My original sixty nine boxes had shrunk to around fifty. Most of those books had been sold on the ferries: but not all. They were also selling in the shops in the south of England. I was being asked for replacements. Orders were also coming through from the 're-order' form that I had printed in the back of the book. Readers were writing me very nice letters. All this was very gratifying; but what made me happiest of all was something which was wholly unexpected. I was getting orders from libraries. *And I was getting orders from bookshops that I had not contacted.* How this came about, I don't know. Perhaps shop managers had personally bought a copy on a ferry, maybe readers who had bought in the same place had placed their re-order with their local bookshop.

Whatever the reason, it gave me the courage to tackle more bookshops. I didn't do this on the phone. I found that a rather time-consuming and wearing process. I did a mail-out in a book-trade magazine. This consisted of a copy of the book's cover with the favourable reviews printed on the back. As a result, I was contacted by the more adventurous of booksellers, each of whom ordered anything between a couple and a couple of dozen copies.

Those bookshop managers were heroes (or more likely heroines) every one. They acted, they ordered and because of them there were a few hundred more books on their shelves and a few hundred less on our utility room floor. Ann would be able to get at the washing machine again without having to use crampons. One day soon I would be able to get close enough to the sink to mend that dripping tap. More importantly, I would be able to start feeding the black hole that was our bank account. Thank you. Thank you!

Then I went for the central ordering departments (where they exist!) of the bookshop chains. I had great success with the smaller (half a dozen shops) chains, less so with the big boys. They would be interested, but only when I had a selling record. It's the catch twenty-two of the book trade, and many other fields of life. Success breeds success. Once you've made it, you find lots of new friends. When you're struggling to get there, they don't find you so fascinating.

Apart from that, I had started my own local initiative to sell copies of my magnum opus in France; in Villedieu, Percy, Avranches, Granville, St Lo, and so on. I visited the local newsagents and bookshops. At first I was pretty nervous; I must have looked a furtive creature as I hung around until the shops were empty, pretending to read magazines or books; for all the world like a youth in the chemist's keen to buy contraceptives. The shopkeepers probably felt much the same, for they treated me with a certain coolness at first; but when I explained my mission they were charm itself. I reckon that you find some of the nicest people in the world in bookshops (and libraries).

I must admit I had thought that the French shopkeepers might have been a bit averse to taking a book in English, but not a bit of it. When I explained that it was about Normandy and its people and their way of life, they couldn't have been more helpful. Soon the book and a poster advertising it were to be seen in quite a few windows.

I don't suppose that I would have got the same response if I'd been a furtive Frenchman in an English bookshop ('Excusez-moi, Madamoiselle, would you like to stock my very nice book about Devon? It's in French'); but then, of course, there aren't so many French visitors in the streets of the typical English town as there are English visitors in its French counterpart.

But, as is sometimes the way of life, as one door began slowly to swing open, another was about to slam painfully in my face. As I hinted earlier, estate agency was not faring well of late. Let me correct that. On the grand scale, estate agency was going beautifully. Customers were visiting. Sales were being made. It was only my corner of the profession that was in trouble.

Reg's promise of an office of my own - like Dick's before him - had never been honoured. Finally, he had told me that it never would be. This was because he had learnt from his French 'front man' - the owner of the *Carte Professionnelle* - that for each office, it was necessary to have a holder of the *Carte*.

As the main reason that I'd joined Reg's agency was because he'd promised me my own office, and as I'd already left one agency precisely because they had not honoured the same promise, this did not please me.

However, Reg told me that I could work from home. He would pay for a telephone line, a fax and a photocopier and I could meet the customers there - or in a café. That at least was legal.

Rather than resign from yet another job into which I'd put lots of work, but reaped little reward, you might think that I would have put the best face that I could on the offer and accepted it. And I might have, had it not been for that telephone call from my friend, the notaire. That phone call (and by the way, my telephone really is a 1940's bakelite one) put a new and very much darker complexion on things.

The article in the *Manche Libre* that I had been advised to read - on the front page - concerned an English agent who had, in conjunction with notaires, been selling houses to the British. I read the piece with mounting amazement and shock. The poor fellow had been given a four month prison sentence for selling property without the benefit of a *Carte Professionnelle*. He had been working from his home in Villedieu. He also received a heavy fine, the bulk of that fine being shared out among local immobiliers as compensation for lost earnings.

The notaires with whom he had worked had not been punished in any way. Which is to say that the only person in the affair who could feasibly claim ignorance of French law (notaires have a degree in the subject) was the only one punished. There's law and there's justice.

The article concentrated my mind wonderfully; and led me quite quickly to quit estate agency altogether. I don't want to go into great detail about this. It's a painful subject. I'm not keen on the sight of blood - especially my own - even though it has dried long ago. Let me merely state that it was not a decision that I took lightly; but only after thorough research and a discussion - at my instigation - with the department at the *Préfecture* (County Hall) which deals with estate agent registration.

I learned from this meeting that unless I travelled into Brittany to pick up my customers I would be breaking the law. (In which case, I had already broken it several times, although I did not see fit to tell the authorities so.) Whereas In Brittany an employee of an estate agency can (according to Reg, I have not verified this with the relevant legal authorities) legally meet clients at his or her home, or at a Café, in 'my' bit of Normandy, neither were legal. The customer and agent must meet at the agency prior to visiting properties.

I passed this information on to Reg, by fax. For his further education, I included a translation of a document which I had obtained from the Prefecture which set out the prerequisites needed for holding the *Carte*.

Reg rang me straight away.

"You didn't mention any names, I hope."

"No."

"Do they have a motto up at the Prefecture? 'You can't keep a good man down - so lock him up instead.'"

"Very funny Reg."

"Yeah, I know; but it's crazy. Where's the logic in it? What's the point in forcing every visitor to report to an estate agency before taking him out? It's just wasting time. You can't tell me that French agents don't meet their customers at properties, or cafes, all the time. How do they intend to police it? Put a tail on every estate agent to make sure that he doesn't meet people outside work? What are they going to ban next? Telephone calls? Advertising in the newspapers? This isn't justice. It's a witch hunt."

Reg was getting worked up. The same thoughts had occurred to me, but I said nothing. After a while, my ex-boss calmed down. There was silence for a while. Then I said: "Have you anything else you would like to say to me, Reg?"

He reflected for a moment. "Can I ask you a question Alan?"

"Sure."

"If we were in Britain, would you have expected two different counties to have two different laws?"

"No. It doesn't make sense to me either."

"And you know that my French isn't up to visiting the Prefecture."

"I trusted you Reg!" I snapped.

There was silence for a while. Then he said "sorry."

There are two kinds of sinner in this world of ours - those of us who think we are already perfect and those who are capable of redemption. Whether we can use that little word is a good start in telling us apart.

I gave Reg a condensed but forcible instruction on the necessity of understanding French law before making job offers based on it. He continued to apologise. Eventually I accepted that apology. He said that he did not want to lose me and suggested that I move down to Brittany. I declined the offer. He asked me what my plans were. The call ended amicably. All very adult. (I'm sure that the reader will not be surprised to learn that my three bosses were not really called 'Reg', 'Dick' or 'Monsieur Pierrot').

What were my plans? If I'd been single, they would probably at that moment have been to throw myself in front of the nearest bus. Instead I was short with Ann, snappy with the kids and shouted at the dog. Then I went over the road and got drunk on René's Calvados. Sorry family. Thanks René.

I had a ticklish time explaining - and apologising to - Bernard. From being a bit of an Anglophone when I first met him, I think he now regards Englishmen as being on an even lower level than Parisians. I could have explained to him that our trouble wasn't a clear-cut thing, but that we had been caught in the devil's own mix of ignorance, self-interest and sledge-hammer law. To my mind, the English in the affair were guilty of the least of those failings.

That was my take on it. I wouldn't be surprised if someone else was also thinking along similar lines. As he slopped out his prison cell. I didn't say any of this to Bernard. Just apologised. My Breton friend had had little enough from me. If he preferred to see life in black and white, what right had I to spoil his vision?

Could I still work selling property?

A reading of the document which set out the requirements for the *Carte Professionnelle* raised the possibility that I might be able to run my own agency.

Back in England only a couple of years earlier, I had designed and implemented for the Government the first computerised system for the sale of council houses to their tenants, a system which had subsequently handled thousands of sales. That might well qualify me. No! Even if it were possible (and it was a big if), the process would take too long.

What about touring the local estate agencies looking for a job? No! I am a very persistent man, but, given enough pain, even I learn to give up. I had been on that reef twice already. A third time would probably drown me. Worse, I would drag my family down with me. Where French property was concerned, I felt that fate was not so much toying with me as dragging me down a flight of concrete steps feet first. For the same reason, I dropped the idea of the *Marchand de Biens*.

The blow was hard, and not only to the pocket and the spirit. Although I had stumbled into the estate agency business by accident, as a stopgap while I studied for my exams, it was a job that I had come to love. I was pretty good at it too (except, as I explained in the last chapter, when faced with customers such as the butcher from Birmingham.)

Although I am a dull-as-a-stick computer type, and my original intention in studying for my French degree had been to use the qualification in order to give me an edge in that profession, I found estate agency much more interesting. I like people, I like to give good service, and I am endlessly fascinated by property.

Maybe it's something in my genes. I remember at school my English teacher telling me that 'Biggin' is Norse, or Danish for buildings; so 'Biggin Hill' simply means building on the hill. Perhaps one of my ancestors jumped out of the longboat and, while his fellows were happily torching and slinging maidens over their shoulders, exclaimed to no one in particular: "I say, what a fine example of early Saxon vernacular architecture!" - only to be pulled back to earth by the riposte: "Eh you, *Biggins* - yes, that's what we'll have to call you from now on - stop farting about and give us a hand looting this monastery."

If I was not to work in estate agency, what else could I do? Although we had originally budgeted that I might not earn any money until I passed my exams, we could not live on fresh air and promises indefinitely. But unemployment is high and jobs hard to come by in rural France.

Should I get more people on to my course? Finding the customers wouldn't have been difficult and I knew that the information that I had collected - the sum knowledge of over a hundred peoples' experiences good and bad - could save an awful lot of people an awful lot of suffering, both financial and emotional. That was a worthwhile job if ever there was one. Only now that I had had first-hand experience of how much it hurt to go onto a reef did I appreciate just how worthwhile. Although I've done little bad in my life, I can't say that I've done a huge amount of good either. In terms of helping others, the course was undoubtedly the most useful job that I had ever done.

But there were problems. My (unpaid) helpers were drifting away. Mike was returning to England (another one!) As the selling season kicked in, Peter was increasingly busy with his real job. I certainly wasn't qualified to lecture on property surveying or legal matters.

I was determined, however, that the knowledge I had gained from the course should not be lost. (And it hasn't been. As it is as interesting as it is valuable, I have used it in this book.)

We (or more correctly, I) thought for a while of running a tea shop in Villedieu (It's virtually impossible to get a decent cup of tea in France, and yet it is crawling with British tourists). Organise cycling holidays? Run a language course? A dozen plans and schemes went through our, or rather my, head; each more crazy than the last. Those were dark days as I struggled to find a way to get out of the mire. I owe Ann a great deal for suffering me during my madness.

Could we even stay in France? We loved Normandy and the kids were happily settled in school, and obviously we must stay until I had finished my exams, but what of the longer term? It looked as though we would have to abandon ship. At least in England I would have more chance of work.

The first thing was to put the house on the market. There was no saying how long it would take to sell the place, although I knew from inside experience that it could be a very long time. So we put our home up for sale. What had I done to my family? What fools we'd been to buy when there was so much property available to rent in the area!

By now it was May and time for my visit to Holloway College in London to take my French exams. (I don't know why women are in general better at languages and men at computing. Maybe it has something to do with the dominant side of the brain. Whatever the cause, there are very few men in computing who can speak a foreign language, and the overwhelming number of people in that industry are men.)

I had passed three out of the four modules necessary to earn the coveted (by me!) Diploma in Foreign Languages of The Institute of Linguists. Now I had to pass the final exam.

My mistake on my previous attempt had been to go for the 'Grand slam'; to take and pass all four modules in one go. I had nearly pulled it off, but I had failed one, the translation from French into English. As one has a choice of six modules, I was determined this time to take two of them at the same time, in the hope that I would thereby pass one.

The two I was going for were the translation from French into English - that is, a repeat of the one which I had previously failed - and an oral.

I love London. I have walked through the capital on hundreds of occasions (I hate tubes) and it gives me a real buzz. From Euston to the Imperial War Museum, from Hammersmith to Woolwich, I have tramped the city up and down, and I love it dearly.

I have stood at the spot where Samuel Pepys watched the fire, viewed the church where he is buried through Dickens' eyes (or prose at least), and eaten the best breakfast known to man at Smithfield. I have gazed affectionately at the oriel window in Saint Bartholomews' church while listening to the choir practising their carols for Christmas, bowed my head where they butchered William Wallace and watched the river pound in spate through the overhanging branches of a lime tree at Westminster. I have drunk at the other Samuel's pub (and it hasn't changed much since his day), and many more beside.

I love the city (or cities) and so it was with pleasure that I got myself into shape on the morning of my exams by walking from Waterloo Station along the south bank of the Thames to Tower Bridge, then along the north bank past the moored boats to Waterloo Bridge (which, as it is on the curve, is my favourite of all the London bridges), before looping back to the college.

As expected, the walk got my brain going and I had no great problems with the translation. The oral was a different story. The subject was capital punishment. I had been talking French day in and day out for over a year, so I thought myself pretty fluent. But I've always been better thinking on my seat than thinking on my feet, and I stumbled when discussing death.

For some reason, the verb *mourir* - 'to die' - would not come to me. I fudged around it somehow, talking about hanging and suicide, but for a precious moment I found myself foundering. I was not pleased with myself.

Still, the deed was done. Soon, I hoped, I would have the precious piece of paper and that educational 'respectability' that I had lacked all of my life. More importantly, I would have a tool to find a new job.

It was about a week after my return when my old black telephone rang with the second of those phone calls which were to radically change our lives in France.

"*Bonjour, Monsieur Bee-geen, c'est Monsieur Simon a l'appareil.*"

Monsieur Simon? The name was familiar, but I couldn't place it.

"You remember. In Paris. I interviewed you at La Défense a few weeks back. You were a trifle damp, I recall."

I remembered.

"Do you perhaps remember that I was awaiting the approval of the Finance Director before I could offer to employ you?"

I remembered.

"He has agreed. Are you still available?"

The lifeboat did float after all! Thank God!

A week later I started work in Paris.

Part 2: Paris

Contracting. A keystone of French history.
Of Parisians and Paris. A walk in Paris.

And so I arrived for my first morning's work in the computer department of a large manufacturing plant in a town just to the north of Paris. It could hardly have been a greater contrast to rural Normandy.

It's funny how circumstances affect your view of things. In previous contracts, my eye had grown somewhat jaundiced. I would, back then, have been exasperated by my reception. The desk covered with manuals and bits of old junk that had been parked there 'temporarily', the computer that didn't work, the slight atmosphere of 'can this guy cut the mustard' mistrust, although normal for day one of a contract, would have annoyed me.

This time I was deliriously happy. I was doing a job which I'm very good at doing and which I enjoy. What was more important, I was unlikely to be put in jail for doing it; and I was getting well paid too!

Computer contractors are employed by companies to provide a short-term resource (typically three months to a year), for example to implement a new computer system, or perhaps to fix a creaky old one.

The contractor himself (as I've said, most are men) has two distinguishing features. Firstly, he does not understand the photocopier. If there's some guy standing over the copier with six doors open, winding frantically on a sprocket, chances are that he's your contractor. If he's snuffling into a hanky, you can be sure of it, for the second attribute which marks him out from his fellow workers is that he will drag himself in to work no matter what a wheezing, spluttering, infection-area he happens to be. The reason is simple enough. If he doesn't work, he doesn't get paid. It's a good life if you don't weaken.

Computer contracting gives one a perhaps unique insight into modern big business. There are various circular themes to be seen in industry which are very educational in a 'Zen and the art of motor-cycle maintenance' kind of way. One of these is centralisation and diversification.

Every few years, the typical centralised company will decide that it is time to split itself up and delegate power to its constituent parts. This calls for lots more computers and systems, so that each subsidiary can control its own destiny. Some time later, a new Chief Executive Officer will decide that this is wasteful, bring everything into central control and replace all the wasteful, unconnected systems with a new central one. Hooray! Says the computer contractor.

The company I was contracting for was in the centralisation phase. As is also common with multi-nationals, it had just been absorbed by another multi-national; a process similar to a succession of ever-larger fish eating each other until a killer whale swallows the one that remains. Of course, that whale is always being circled by sharks eager to rip it to pieces...

The work that I was employed to do was to analyse the company's order processing and accounting systems (there were eleven of them in seven different countries), and work out what the interfaces between the different processes should be. Then I was to help to implement the new system and specify new programs where necessary.

The pay-off for the American mother company was that their head office would then be able to see where their money was being earned and spent. They would also save a lot of money by not needing so many computers world-wide.

I was also to lead a project to design the European communications network, specifically in the core plants in England and France.

The contract was interesting. My time was to be split roughly between England and France (with odd visits to other countries). One of the teams that I was managing was French; in the computer department of the large manufacturing plant in the town just to the north of Paris.

But I will leave my work-related stories of derring-do in the Accounts Department, and heroic and hard-fought victories which I have won over recalcitrant TCP/IP and SNA protocols, for another day (or, if you are lucky, never). Because they're boring, and anyway that's quite enough about me, and more than enough about computing! Instead, I'd like to talk about

Paris.

Paris was born on the Ile de la Cité when the Parisii tribe settled there in the third century B.C. The *Ile* is an easily defended island at what was at that time a ford in the Seine. The hills of Montmarte rise to the north (Right Bank), while to the south (Left Bank), is the Montagne Sainte Geneviève.

Paris (or Lutetia as it was known to the Romans), seems to have been much loved. The Emperor Julian described it as:

"My dear Lutetia, a small island enclosed within the walls of its ramparts, accessible through two wooden bridges alone."

The post-Roman history of France has much in common with that of England in that in both cases they were over-run by Germanic tribes. In France's case, these were predominantly the Franks from around Frankfurt. In the early sixth century, Clovis, king of the Franks, established the seat of his realm in Paris.

As an understanding of the consequences of the 'German connection' is key to an understanding of much of modern France, I will follow this strand of history a little further ('Left Bank' and 'Right Bank', for example, only make sense if you're coming from the east). If you are allergic to history - as many people are - please feel free to 'fast-forward' a page or two.

The major differences between the Germanic invasions of England and France was that the Angles, Saxons and Danes brought their own languages with them to England and seem to have killed or driven out the Celts almost completely. The Franks, on the other hand, lived with the Gauls, adopted their language and became their rulers.

The empire of Charlemagne, a later King of the Franks,

covered most of continental Europe. After his death, that empire was split - more or less - into France and Germany. The French covered-up their German antecedents for many centuries. In 1714, Nicholas Fremiet was imprisoned in the Bastille for three months for saying that the Franks were a German tribe. A little later, the Count of Bolanvilliers in his *Nobility of France* (1732) upheld the claim, saying that the privileges of the nobility were justified because there were two populations in France, in fact two races. The masters, who were Germanic and the serfs who were Gallic.

While this may have been true in terms of conquerors and conquered, it was possibly a little arrogant, perhaps even imprudent, to state it publicly. When, sixty years later, the French Revolution broke out in Paris and the necks of *le deuxième état* began to feel the touch of the guillotine, the theory was neatly turned against those nobles by the French historians of the early nineteenth century, who justified the savagery of the revolution by claiming it as a racial (anti-Germanic) war. An early example of the justification of mass murder as 'ethnic cleansing'.

(As a cultural sidelight, I must point out that the guillotine - which remained in use in France until 1976 - was actually a Yorkshire invention. It was invented in Halifax twenty years before the French revolution and copied by Doctor Guillotine. From this fact springs the Yorkshire couplet 'From Hell, Hull and Halifax, may the good lord preserve us.' I'm not sure why Hull; and maybe it's not much to be proud of, but there it is!)

After Napoléon's defeat at Waterloo (which Wellington attributed to pre-match planning on the playing fields of Eton, but which might also have had something to do with Bonaparte's piles, or the appearance of a Prussian army under Blucher), Paris saw a number of revolutions. The last of these was in

195

1870 - as the result of the invasion of France by Prussia - and led to the abolition of the French monarchy.

The 'siege mentality', caused by the Prussian invasion of 1870 and heightened greatly by the further German invasions of 1914 and 1940, has had significant physical effects on France (lots of defences). What is less obvious, but every bit as profound, is the effect that it has had on the French psyche.

End of history lesson!

You may think that this is a bit steep coming from a Yorkshireman, but I find one of the most annoying characteristics of (some of) the French to be an uncritical (yet curiously defensive) praise of their own institutions, language, fashion and food. The French themselves make mock of this complacent crowing, one of the emblems of France being the '*Coq Gaulois*', a vain, strutting, dung-heap cock.

Nowhere is this insular vanity more pronounced than in Paris. So when they describe their capital as 'The City of Light', 'Cultural capital of the world' and so forth, there is a very natural tendency among the more self-effacing inhabitants of our islands to take this as merely the bombastic blusterings of a braggart. The trouble is, of course, that Paris is wonderful, is marvelous, is magical. Damn.

The best way to get to know Paris (or anywhere else for that matter) is to walk through it. And Paris is a great city for a walk. Of the major cities that I know (not an exhaustive list), it's the best. That's partly because it is unusually walker-friendly.

In London, which is two cities (Westminster and London) side by side, attractions are often very wide apart. For instance, the museums of South Kensington are six or seven miles from the Tower of London, while - as far as tourist attractions are concerned - St Paul's Cathedral is virtually stuck out on its own. To join up the dots you're more or less forced to take the tube.

America is even worse. New York stretches forever along Manhattan Island, and its grid system, in serving its function of distributing traffic evenly, also makes it more difficult to walk across the city. Las Vegas worships the car to such a point that large areas of the town have no pavements at all. When walking in American towns, I get the feeling that I am a second-class citizen, simply because I'm not consuming as I go.

Paris is different. It's not that the drivers are nice. Far from it. You only have to try and cross the road in the Place de la République, with the traffic coming from eight directions at once, like a hive of enraged hornets, weaving, hooting, drivers leaning out of their windows to snarl, the whole ignoring police, traffic lights and pedestrian crossings (*bien sur*), to realise that, put behind the wheel, the average Parisian becomes a selfish and unimaginative dullard who, in a fair society, would be arrested, spot-fined and sentenced to repaint lines on pedestrian crossings for a year.

No, the beauty of Paris is that its centre is human-scale and relatively small. Most of it (or at least most of the bits the tourist usually visits) is in an area of three miles by two. Into that small span is packed one of the world's greatest - and most beautiful - cities.

The Sunday walk through Paris that Ann and I have planned is to be a pleasure rather than a route-march. Although we will hardly even scratch the surface of what Paris has to offer, yet we will see much. Now the day has arrived.

I think each member of the family has a slightly different agenda for our walk. Mine is to stretch my legs, see what's happening, look at the city and hang out with the family. Ann also wants to visit an art gallery or two. Alice wants to look at the shops (what kind of consumer-child have I sired here!). David is 'just following orders'; although a burger or toys would be a very definite plus.

Our starting point was to have been a trip up the Eiffel Tower. We get there early, but not early enough. One look at the queue snaking under the Tower is enough to tell us that. So we wander up to the Arc de Triomphe instead, Napoléon's arch to celebrate bashing up the Russians or some such. Then we walk down the Champs Elysées towards the Place de la Concorde. As we walk, I lecture the family about Haussman (the man who designed and constructed the Avenues and Boulevards of modern Paris in the 1850's):

"Notice, children, the regularity of the boulevards; and their width. Designed by Baron Haussman under Napoléon the Third. A perfect example of French centralised planning. The Baron bulldozed most of the old city to build them. And they're wide so that the army could control them with cannons. The Parisians are a very revolutionary crowd."

I always think that my history lectures have a two-fold advantage. Not only do they impart knowledge; they make the kids walk faster. I am up with them though, piqued by their lack of interest and feigning revenge.

"You had your fun yesterday, at Disneyland. Today's culture!"

"I told you we should have taken the Métro, Alan. The kids will get soaked."

"It's only a shower love. Toughen them up!" But I am talking to myself. The three of them are off, dashing for the stairs into a nearby Métro station. It is one of those sudden heavy spring downpours that bounce the rain a foot off the pavements and soak you within seconds. In a continental deluge like this, it's hard to believe that Paris's annual rainfall is only an inch more than London's. We stand on the steps with a dozen others as the dark sky unloads its torrents, brief comrades, laughing with the exhilaration of it all.

We cheat a bit here and take the Métro a couple of stops to the Louvre, that old royal palace by the Seine turned magnificent museum. I know that Ann is aching to look round the place, but the kids are 'anti', which in turn makes me less than keen (with the kids in such a mood, the chances of Ann and I getting anything from the experience except irritation and guilt is, in my opinion, of a very low order). So we cross onto the Ile de la Cité and visit the cathedral of Notre Dame (where Napoléon crowned *himself*). This is a safe bet. There is something for everyone here. We climb up onto the roof and look at the gargoyles. *Quelle imagination*! Such wonderful, wild and whimsical beasts stare out over the rooftops of the city to the distant hills. And what a view!

After Notre Dame we visit the excavations beneath the *Parvis*, a word that has no equivalent in English, but which is, according to my French dictionary:

'an area which extends before the principal entrance of a church, from low Latin *paradisus*, Greek *paradis*'.

It's not paradise down there, it's dark and atmospheric. Here, where Paris was founded, are revealed layer upon layer, from Roman times to the Nineteenth Century: the remains of streets, wells, rooms, walls, windows. An eerie, exciting place. A cross-section of the city preserved beneath the rubbish which has buried and hidden it over the years, just as we, as individuals, are apt, in time, to lose our own true forms beneath the rubbish that we accumulate.

Then we cross over onto the smaller and quieter Ile St

Louis. Here you are far from Haussman's Paris - the grand capital of empire - and into a more French and human place. The island seems quite cut-off and has the feel of one of those quiet, ancient and slightly down-at-heel provincial towns. There's money here, that's for certain, but money which doesn't feel the need to prove anything. There are crumbling stone walls with tempting gates that lead to who-knows-what secret gardens and big old doors with an interesting line in door-knockers (a minor interest of mine).

On this island we come upon a trinket shop. The girls like that. David is less keen, but it is me who ends up buying something. It is a cast-iron model of one of those Gothic Parisian newspaper kiosks. I love Parisian street furniture; it is so stylish and unmistakably French (although as the French call such structures *Colonnes Morris* - Morris Columns - they're probably not a French invention at all, but the product of the fertile brain of that champion of decorative arts, William Morris, of Essex and Hammersmith).

Further along the street we come upon a newsagent. We all want to go in. Ann loves stationery. I like old shops and old shopkeepers. Alice has spotted a 'Tintin' annual she doesn't have. David has a special mission.

It is the kind of shop that you used to find in the back streets of English towns when I was a boy. Dark, dependable, with a sign which usually seemed to say 'Closed, even for the sale of Senior Service.' It has modern stuff; displays of postcards, guidebooks, envelopes and paper, toys and so on - but you feel as if this is only a veneer, a camouflage for the real business that goes on here. That is represented by the shelves (which stretch all the way up to the lofty ceiling). These are certain-sure to contain anything that has been anything in stationery during the last century.

Above all, this is the kind of place you would want to find if you suddenly found yourself short of sealing-wax, or string, or tie-on luggage labels, or brown paper. Or caps for your capgun. Which is what David asks for.

The lady produces a plastic circle of about a dozen caps. No! That isn't it at all! Too expensive. Not enough caps! What David is after is a paper roll (always red or green) of a hundred caps.

"Ah yes!" The owner smiles nostalgically. "I know what you mean. Haven't seen those for years. Wait a moment!" She shuffles off into the back and returns in triumph. *"Tu as de la chance, jeune homme."*

And David *is* lucky. He gets such a supply of caps as will keep him going for months. Alice gets her *Tintin* book, Ann her postcards, while I pick up an interesting book: *Paris, des origines à nos jours.*

Then we cross over to the Left Bank and wander through the mass of medieval streets which is the Latin Quarter, which gets its name from the days when the inhabitants of this, the university area, spoke Latin as their first language. I briefly pop into 'Shakespeare and Company', a most remarkable second-hand bookshop owned by a gentleman called George Whitman, an American who is living proof that charity is alive and well in the modern age. Here in Paris, within sight of Notre Dame, Mr. Whitman allows (or did at the time) travelers to sleep above his shop for an hour's work a day.

We are heading for the Arab Institute, a tall modern building which stands by the side of the Seine. The window-blinds of this building are like camera apertures, designed to open and close themselves in response to the intensity of sunlight. Fascinating to watch. There, high above Paris and the river, we had planned to have our luncheon. But it is not to be.

201

Somewhere, we go astray and end up far from our destination. Not that it matters. We have had a good look round and sampled not a few shops; and we are still in an interesting area. Nearby there is the Panthéon (burial place of some of France's greatest citizens whose permanent guests include Voltaire, Jean-Jacques Rousseau, Louis Braille, Emile Zola, Jean Moulin and Pierre and Marie Curie) and the Roman Baths. But we are a bit 'monumented out' now, and getting hungry. The road is a very quiet one, bordered by trees. We flop into seats outside a promising café-restaurant.

The service is somewhat slow. The smell from a cabinet of roasting chickens increases our hunger.

"Smells good, doesn't it David?"

Ann says: "If the waiter doesn't come soon, we'll just have to live on the smell."

"They might still charge us."

"Don't be silly, dad."

"Well, I reckon they might, you know. They've tried it before in the Latin Quarter, in that street we were in earlier, you know, the one where I told you that Napoléon used to live?"

"No."

"The one where I showed you the little street with the funny name."

"Oh yes," puts in Alice, "*La Rue du chat qui peche*".

"Yes that's right - the street of the Fishing Cat, the one which used to go down to the Seine before they built the embankment - I think that it's the narrowest street in Paris. Anyway, the street that it leads off, the Rue de la Huchette; that's where they used to charge for the whiff of a meal."

"Come on!"

"No, it's true; or according to Rabelais it is, anyway."

"Rabelais?"

"A great French writer. Maybe the greatest. Anyway, the Rue de la Huchette was once famous for its spit-roasted meats. Rabelais says that such a lovely smell of roasting filled the street that many a poor devil who could not afford to buy would visit it, including the porters who worked on the other side of the river. They would troop across the Seine at meal-times just for the pleasure of eating their crusts in the delightful aroma."

At last a waiter appears. Alice asks for *crepes sucrés,* David goes for something and chips, I go for steak (will I never learn?), Ann opts for a salad.

"*Et pour boire?*"

Two Oranginas for the children, a glass of red wine for Ann. I want a glass of fresh milk; something almost impossible to get hold of in France, where U.H.T. is the dreadful norm. Consequently I stress that the *lait* must be *frais* - fresh. The waiter looks mystified, but I insist.

"Dad the great linguist." Puts in David rudely as the waiter leaves. "You even speak French with a Yorkshire accent!"

"Nonsense! You'd think I was a native."

"Of Barnsley maybe!" Ann cuts in.

They're ganging up on me.

"Can I get on with my story? ...and so it was that a labourer was eating his bread by the fumes of a roast, which made it more tasty. The *rotisseur* made no objection, but when the bread was eaten, he seized the porter by the collar and insisted that the latter paid him for the fumes of the roast."

The children gasp at the enormity of this.

"The porter insisted that he had in no way damaged the meat, that he had taken nothing and therefore owed nothing. The fumes in question evaporated and were lost; never had a case been heard in Paris of the smell of a roast being sold in the street."

"I should think not!" Scoffs Alice. "Then what happened?"

"Well, the *rotisseur* cut up rough. He said that he wasn't obliged to feed porters with the fumes of his roast. He swore that if the fellow didn't pay he would beat the money out of him. The porter seized a stick and prepared to defend himself. What a to do! The noodles of Paris gathered from all points of the compass to be in on it! In the crowd, as luck would have it, was Seigny Joan, the Fool, Citizen of Paris."

"The fool?"

"Don't be silly, David. The Fool. The jester. Go on dad."

"So the *rotisseur* asked the porter if he would accept the judgement of the noble Seigny Joan on the dispute. The porter agreed."

"Then Seigny Joan, after having heard what they had to say, commanded the porter to draw a piece of silver from his belt. The porter did so. Seigny Joan took the coin and put it on his shoulder as if to test its weight; then he tapped it on the counter to make sure that it rang true; then he placed it to his eye as though he wanted to see that it was properly stamped. All this was done in great silence in the midst of the staring people, while the *rotisseur* waited in supreme confidence and the porter in despair. Finally, Seigny Joan struck the piece of silver several more times on the counter."

"Like this," volunteers David, striking a coin against the table top.

"That's it son. Then with the majesty of a judge, holding his bauble as though it had been a sceptre, and muffling his head in his hood of apes' fur, with paper for ears, with a frill about his neck stuck out like organ pipes, the Fool coughed loudly two or three times and pronounced his sentence:

"'The Court declares that the porter who has eaten his

bread by the fumes of the roast has legally paid the *rotisseur* with the sound of his money. The said Court further decrees that each return to his own home, without cost or redress.' So, my children, you must consider the wisdom of asking advice of a fool."

"Or have one take you to a restaurant!" Puts in Ann in exasperation. "How am I to write my postcards with this going on? And what about the one you're supposed to be writing to your mother?"

So we settle down to wait. David and Alice with *Tintin*, me with my *History of Paris*, Ann with her postcards. I am feeling quite happy. I know of no other city (except perhaps Venice) where I would rather have spent the day with my family.

Five minutes later the drinks arrive. Instead of the *lait frais* which I have commanded, I am presented (with much ceremony) with *un lait fraise* a strawberry milkshake, complete with its own umbrella on a stick.

It seems, as my family are not slow to point out, that Alan Biggins, computer contractor and linguist *extraordinaire*, has made a mistake.

Although I hold it my duty to support my family, I must own that there are times when I find them completely insupportable.

SELLING FRENCH DREAMS

A family journey.
Brennt Paris? Three candles.

"I don't know any city where the past is
involved with the present as much as in
Paris." (Kitty Beaurepos)

When I travel from London to Paris, I prefer to drive. Flying has
too much potential for delay. By the time that you've driven to
the airport, waited for the plane, flown, waited to clear customs
and found a taxi, you're several hours in the red. The train is
superb, but limits the amount that you can carry. I often take
equipment back and forth.

Driving also gives me the chance to listen to music, the music that I like, as loud as I like. The M25 round London even has its very own song:
"This ain't no technological breakthrough.
This is the road to hell."

The road to Hell describes the London orbital pretty well, with its hold-ups, queues, bumper hugging and wall-to-wall lorries. But I rarely listen to anything on the M25. I'm a nervous driver and I'm too busy just staying in one piece. It is when I roll off the train at Calais that I click in a cassette, put my foot down and go.

The way that life has changed in my lifetime is astonishing. I was born in Kirkbymoorside, a fairly remote red-tiled small town on the edge of the Yorkshire Moors, in 1953. Although the sun never set on the British Empire and great chunks of the map of the world were still coloured red, there were still people in my part of the world who had spent their whole life without having been to York, twenty- six miles away. Yet here I am, having left England an hour back, headed towards Paris on a routine journey. I am to deliver and install an Andrews Active Star. Not a shooting star, such as the one I saw in Brittany. A small piece of communications equipment in a network which will link Germany, France, Britain and America.
I pull onto the motorway and take a ticket at the toll booth. Then I turn the tape on full and put my foot down.
Meatloaf blares out:
"Like a bat outta hell, I'll be gone when the morning comes, comes, comes..."

I am heading for Arras, where I shall turn right - south - to

Paris. The main road to Paris largely follows the trenches of the First World War; where the troops of Britain and her empire fought alongside those of France against Germany.

In a sense, although I am alone in the car, it is a family journey. Among the Biggins men folk at least. For I'm far from being the first with my name to be in this bit of France. My grandfather came this way too, to fight in the trenches of the Somme in the Great War. The 'war to end all wars', a war which, unlike Waterloo, was all-but-lost on the playing fields of Eton, for the chief lesson the Wall Game (a muddy scrum in which the last goal was scored in 1909) taught the English officers, attrition, was not much use in the 1914-18 war.

While showing fortitude in a jumbled mass of bodies might have been a good way of knocking the imagination out of the upper classes, it was not an ideal education for future generals in dealing with the facts of modern European war.

Over the top on the whistle, through a shell-scarred lunar landscape into the fire of the waiting machine guns. No subtlety, no fore-play. Drown the enemy by numbers. The bankrupt philosophy of repeated frontal attacks which cost one hundred thousand British casualties in 1915.

"What passing bells for those that die as cattle?
Only the monstrous anger of the guns.
Only the stuttering rifles' rapid rattle,
can patter out their hasty orisons"
(Wilfred Owen. Anthem for doomed youth)

There were another one hundred and twenty thousand British and Canadian casualties in 1917. In the view of the Germans, the British troops were 'lions led by donkeys'.

The tape turns over. It's a compilation. I generally fast-forward through the next track, which is 'Sabre Dance' by Love Sculpture. It's too wild to drive to.

I'm driving over the sites of the battlefields now. They still yield their harvest of death from a war nearly a century old. Twenty tons of shells, half of them gas, are dug up and must be disposed of every year.

Here, across the route of this road between Arras and Rheims, in the spring of 1918 the German army came out of the east to make its last great attack of the war. It pushed thirty miles forward and to within thirty miles of Paris. The Germans were desperate to win before the new American armies fully entered the war. When the counter-attack came, they didn't have the strength to hold. On August the eighth, the Allies rolled through the German start line. The German commander called it 'the black day of the German army'.

The signposts off the road, Vimy, Bapaume, Cambrai, also point the way to the graves of many tens of thousands of British soldiers. They represent the death of a generation.

The track blaring from my cassette player very nearly proves prophetic:
"Don't you know baby,
we're standing on the eve of destruction."

I'm catching up too fast with a knackered old Citroen 2CV, oily smoke pouring out of its exhaust.

I've been rolling south for a while now. The *Train de Grande Vitesse* appears, rolls past with a whoosh and disappears. There is definitely something to be said for the train. I'm getting a little tired. It will do me good to get out for a walk when I get to Paris.

I pass the turning to Compiègne. There, on November 11th 1918, in a railway carriage in a clearing in the forest, the Germans surrendered.

I'm running low on fuel. Must top-up before Paris.

The Germans came back, of course, in 1940, when their troops marched around the end of the 'impregnable' Maginot Line (which ended at the Belgian border) and broke through at Sedan. Again.

The French, bled white in the first war, and riddled with corruption and defeatism, had not prepared for a second war. They were not alone in that, but they did not have the Channel to defend them. Despite local resistance (of which de Gaulle was the most celebrated example), the Germans quickly broke through. Back in that clearing at Compiègne, in the same railway carriage in which the German surrender had been signed in 1918, Hitler took the French surrender in 1940. Then he burned the railway carriage. He must have had doubts, even then.

I am leaving the old front line behind. My trip in my grandfather's footsteps is over. Not just in the footsteps of my grandfather, of course; but in those of half the men of Europe, America and the British Empire. Many of them still lie here. I stop at the toll booth, tender my ticket and pay the toll. I switch off the cassette. Now for the horrors of the Périphérique - the Paris ring-road. I don't listen to music on that road either.

I'm not taking the most direct route to my job in central Paris. I'm going to park out of town and walk in. Not that I'm malingering. Perish the thought! When I'm abroad and away from my family, I tend to work late in the evenings. Today, in fact, I have to do so, for the Andrews Active Star can only be fitted after hours, when no-one is using the computer network (if I can ever get the users to sign off!)

In the previous chapter, I gave a couple of reasons why Paris is such a great city to walk in. I should also have mentioned another: the fact that it still has an historic city centre, rather than having been blown to kingdom-come during the war, as were so many other European cities. Only lately have I found out why that is the case. The answer was given me by a book that I've been reading called 'Is Paris Burning' (by Larry Collins and Dominique Lapierre), which is about the liberation of Paris in 1944; and that book has suggested the route for my walk today.

With the Normandy landings of June 6th 1944, the liberation of their capital seemed very close to the French people. The Allied high command, however, did not see the freeing of Paris as an immediate objective. Fighting for a city can mean the destruction of that city, as the examples of Warsaw and Stalingrad had recently shown. Besides, it looked as if the Germans meant to blow Paris sky-high. They had a vast stockpile of explosives in the city. The torpedoes for the Atlantic U-boat fleet were manufactured there. There were, in the words of one of the engineers:

"Enough torpedoes to shoot two wars through."

And the military commander of the city, General von Choltitz, was just the man to blow The City of Light apart. Von Choltitz, hand-picked by Hitler for the French capital, had already undertaken the destruction of Rotterdam and Sebastopol. He was a 'scorched-earther' *par excellence.* Hitler had ordered him to Paris because: "the only fighting going on there is over the seats in the officers' mess." Von Choltitz was to turn Paris "into a frontline city." He was under Hitler's orders to "stamp out without pity" any resistance.

It looked as if Hitler had made an inspired choice. By D-day, two hundred factories, the Eiffel Tower, the Palais de Luxembourg, the Chamber of Deputies and the Foreign Ministry, as well as the telephone network and all railway stations and bridges, were either already mined or on the list for destruction.

Showing the Swedish Consul, Raoul Nordling, a map of Paris, and jabbing it at random, Choltitz said:

"Suppose a bullet is fired at one of my men, here, on the Avenue de l'Opéra, I would burn down every building in the block, and shoot all the inhabitants."

To do so, he had at his disposal twenty-two thousand troops, mostly SS, a hundred Tiger tanks and ninety aircraft.

Danger was added to this powder keg in that a power struggle was going on within the French Resistance movement. That movement was split into two factions, one supported de Gaulle, the other was Communist. Whichever was victorious would control Paris and therefore France. The Communist group intended to stage an uprising. De Gaulle's commander on the spot saw that if he let the Communists take the lead, he risked losing Paris. On August the 19th, therefore, French Gaullist police occupied their own *Préfecture de Police*.

The Communist-led FFI began to attack isolated German soldiers, and occupied police stations, post offices and the twenty Parisian town halls, among them Neuilly.

The commune of Neuilly bordering the Bois de Boulogne was one of the quietest corners of France. Block for block, its eighteenth century town houses probably lodged more collaborators, Vichyites, German agents and Germans than any other part of Paris.

The Germans, who had already carried out 4,500 executions in Paris, reacted as was to be expected. The Neuilly town hall was attacked by tanks and quickly reoccupied. The surviving defenders were led off (save for some who escaped through that standard Parisian *route d'évasion*, the sewers).

My mind jerks back to the present. Ah yes, Neuilly sur Seine. I'm just going through it now. Two more exits until I leave the ring road.

German tanks began to attack the Prefecture of Police. When von Choltitz ordered more tanks, and aircraft to attack, the Swedish Consul, Raoul Nordling, went to see him. He pointed out that this would probably involve the destruction of much of historic Paris. Von Choltitz, wavering, declared a truce. But he was running scared of his superiors. In a lowered tone he addressed the Swede:

"I have one thing to ask you. Don't associate my name with the truce."

When Jodl, Hitler's Chief of Staff, demanded of von Choltitz if the mined buildings of Paris had been destroyed, the latter replied that the insurrection had stopped him. This was the first that the German High Command had heard of the uprising. Jodl told von Choltitz:

"Whatever happens, the Fuhrer expects you to carry out the widest destruction possible in the area assigned to your command."

Over the next few days, the truce, regarded by the Communists as a betrayal, broke down and fighting worsened in the city. Rol, the leader of the Communists, declared in that way that is all too common with visionaries: "Paris is worth 200,000 dead."

I am pulling off the Périphérique now, entering Hausmann's old Paris by the Porte de Passy. I park the car, take the Andrews Active Star (a small package) from the boot and walk along the Quai de Grenelle, a modern street of high-rise office towers on the south bank of the Seine.

Hundreds did die, including four truckloads of German troops ambushed on the Left Bank. Fire-bombed, burning soldiers ran screaming through the narrow alleys of the medieval quarter.

Von Choltitz was repeatedly urged to carry out the destruction of Paris. But he did nothing. On the 22nd of August, he again summoned Nordling, telling him that he would need 'very soon' to obey Hitler's command to quell the insurrection even if it meant destroying large parts of the city. Speaking slowly and in a very sober tone, he leaned forward and told Nordling that the only thing that might prevent those orders from being carried out was the rapid arrival of the Allies in Paris:

> "You must realise that my behaviour in telling you this could be interpreted as treason. Because what I'm really doing is asking the Allies to help me."

The Swede managed to get through to the Allied lines and the 2nd Armoured Division (Free French) under General le Clerc and the 4th (U.S.) Division were dispatched to Paris. In the meantime, Jodl had ordered more German troops and armour to the French capital. The race was on.

On the 24th August, on Hitler's orders, a Luftwaffe major contacted von Choltitz. He was ready to proceed with the carpet-bombing of Paris. It must be a night attack because of the overwhelming strength of the Allied air-forces. Preferably that night. Von Choltitz responded angrily. It was impossible: how could the bombers differentiate between friend and foe?

I am crossing the Place des martyrs juifs du velodrome d'hiver. Bit of a mouthful that. The Jews of Paris were penned into the velodrome d'hiver - a winter sports pitch - before being shipped off to be murdered. If the first war was a struggle for territory, Hitler's war was evil.

I stop for a moment in thought. I am proud of my people; for it is we, the British, that stood alone against that evil. We could have compromised in 1940, it would have been easy to do so. The temptation was enormous. At the cost of allowing Germany ro keep Europe, Hitler offered us peace. With Russia on Germany's side, and America neutral, it seemed that our only alternative was, as Churchill put it: 'blood, sweat, and tears.' And, in the end, probable defeat. But we chose that dark way: "We will fight them on the beaches, we will fight them in the streets. We will never surrender. If the British Empire lasts a thousand years, men will still say 'this was their finest hour.'" Of course the British Empire didn't last. But it was still our finest hour; and Churchill our finest man. He was the rock against which Hitler could not prevail; he the man who made the liberation of Europe possible.

I also feel proud of the part my father played; he fought from North Africa, right across Europe.

On the 25th of August 1944, the Free French Division

fought its way into Paris. The same day, Hitler demanded of Jodl:

"*Brennt Paris*?" - Is Paris burning?
A silence fell on the bunker.
"Jodl." Hitler repeated, smashing his fist on the table. "I want to know - Is Paris burning? Is Paris burning right now, Jodl?"

Paris was not burning. At noon of the day that Hitler posed the question, the tricolour was flying again over the Eiffel Tower, for the first time since the 13th of June 1940.

The Eiffel Tower rises majestically above me. I have walked through a largely modern area; but now I'm into true Paris bourgeois. Tall sheer houses of six or seven stories, french windows on each floor leading out to cast-iron balconies, the whole topped off by steep slate roofs. I cross the Seine and continue on the north side. A ten minute walk leads me to the Arc de Triomphe.

I have caught up with my story. Shortly after the tricolour was hoisted over the Eiffel Tower, an extraordinary tank duel took place here. Where I am standing, at the Arc end, was a Sherman of the 2nd Armoured Division, the *Simoun.* Three shells were fired at it from a Panzer tank in the Place de la Concorde, a mile to the east at the other end of the Champs Elysées. The first shell tore off the last gaslight in the broad avenue. Two more sailed over the *Simoun.* The first chipped off the base of the statue of the Marseillaise. The second plunged under the largest triumphal arch in the world and the tomb of France's Unknown Soldier.

The commander of the *Simoun* ordered gunner Robert

Mady to fire at the Panzer, giving him a range of 1,500 metres. Mady clicked off the range on his gunsight. Then he added three more stops. He remembered having read long ago that the length of the Champs Elysées from the Obelisk was 1,800 metres. Mady fired. He was right. The first shot hit the Panzer. Watching a column of grey smoke seep up from the injured tank, Mady suddenly said to himself. "Bon Dieu, if I'd shot two metres to the right, I would have knocked down the Obelisk!"

I walk down the Champs Elysées, wide and perfect for the use of artillery. Designed for the job. Twenty minutes later I am in the Place de la Concorde (It is here that the guillotine operated during the Reign of Terror after the revolution of 1789). I'm nearing the end of my journey now.

The Panzer in the Place de la Concorde was rammed from behind by a Sherman tank and finished off. The Sherman was one of five tanks, the *Mort Homme*, *Douamont*, *Laffaux*, *Montfaucon* and *Villers-Cotteret* which had come along the Rue de Rivoli from the opposite direction, from the east. All were to be damaged or destroyed.

I turn into the Rue Rivoli. Here, in the Hotel Meurice, von Choltitz, Commander of Greater Paris, had his seat of government. This was the objective of the Free French attack.

On that August afternoon in 1944, the shell of the *Mort-Homme* lay outside the Meurice, burnt to ruin by a grenade dropped into its open turret. In front of the Meurice stood Lieutenant Henri Karcher. Seconds before, the lieutenant had had the closest brush with death he had ever known. At the instant he turned his head to pass an order to the soldier behind him, a tracer bullet had singed his left eyebrow. Had his head not been turned, he realised, the bullet would have gone through his eye and into his brain.

Karcher was one of de Gaulle's original few. A Parisian, he had never even seen his son, born on the 3rd of June 1940.

Submachine-gun in hand, Karcher and his three men entered the Meurice. He turned his gun on the huge portrait of Hitler which dominated the lobby. It shattered to bits. A sand-bagged soldier on the first floor landing opened fire on the four men. Karcher replied with a phosphorus grenade. Through the mass of acrid smoke filling the lobby appeared a German officer, his hands in the air. Karcher told him to order his men to surrender. The German complied. An officer in the red-striped trousers of the general staff appeared at the top of the stairs. Karcher sprang forward. "Where," he asked, "is your general?"

As von Choltitz stood on the back of a lorry in the Rue de Rivoli about to be driven into captivity, he watched a sight he would never forget. Behind him a grotesquely ugly Parisienne was dancing a wild jig on the pavement. Over her head she jubilantly flourished her personal trophy of the liberation of this, her city. It was a pair of trousers and down their seams ran the proud claret stripes of a general officer of the Wehrmacht.

But it wasn't quite all over yet. The next day, de Gaulle himself was fired-on, in Notre Dame Cathedral. He showed great bravery. It was never discovered who had fired the shots. De Gaulle was convinced it was the Communists, whom he disarmed at once, striking, as he said, while the iron was hot.

I stand outside the Meurice (*le trés confidential* - you've got to hand it to the French) for a while and think about the main protagonists and how they have affected our world. Of course it was Allied arms, British, American and Soviet, which freed Europe; but the greatest safeguard of peace in our continent is European unification. That unification is the main reason why, unlike those of my father and grandfather, my journey has been in peace; and so will my son David's be. And part of the thanks for that must go to the men who were here on that day in August 1944.

We can certainly thank von Choltitz for his part in making a European union possible. Tried by the Nazis in absentia for dereliction of duty, who can say what motivated the man? An understandable reluctance to blow up the world's cultural capital under the eyes of history and with certain defeat and retribution swiftly approaching? More lofty ideals? Who knows. And yet, he did save Paris. If he had pressed the plunger, there could have been no united Europe, at least probably not in our lifetime.

Von Choltitz was held in a prisoner-of-war camp in the United States until 1947, whereupon he returned to Germany. Snubbed by fellow former officers, he wrote a book, *Brennt Paris?* (1951), in which he defended his disobedience of a leader whom he felt had gone mad. He died in 1966.

If you are wealthy enough to book into the very upmarket Hotel Meurice today, feel free to ask for his suite. He stayed in room 213.

And we owe thanks to de Gaulle. But here we are on even slippier ground. Given that in 1940 Churchill proposed that Britain and France become one nation, the fact that de Gaulle fought tooth and nail to keep Britain out of Europe seems shocking indeed. But then, de Gaulle's aim wasn't so much to unite Europe as to forge a Franco-German superstate on his own terms - while Germany was on the ropes. His move was fuelled by the fact that it had been proved thrice in a century that France could not stand against German might.

De Gaulle claimed to speak for France. In fact, he claimed to *be* France. You have to worry about a man who thinks he is a place. His aim, peace for his country (himself?) by an exclusive alliance with Germany, was too limited. That French dream (or rather that Frenchman's dream) found no buyer. Wiser heads than his could see that the proud General's vision only had a value if the whole of Europe could sleep peacefully in their beds. The way of power-blocs and alliances had spilt enough blood in the old continent already.

I believe that the limitation lay in the man himself. To get an insider's view of him, I can do no better than to quote from an American, Ben Lucien Burman, who was wounded in the trenches in the 1914-18 war, lived in Paris for twenty years, passed the second war as the American Ambassador to the Free French, and was awarded the French Legion of Honour. A good friend of France, but no fan of de Gaulle:

"The actions of de Gaulle himself in recent years can have come as no surprise to those who, like myself, have had an earlier knowledge of his character... ....De Gaulle's shocking rejection of Britain was a logical development of the events through which he was created and the later events detailed in these pages (his book, *The Generals wear cork hats*). Despite all his talk of grandeur, de Gaulle was and is suffering from a terrible inferiority complex. De Gaulle was created by Britain, nourished by Britain, sanctified by Britain. Without Britain in the war de Gaulle as we know him would never have existed; with British aid withdrawn de Gaulle would not have lasted ten minutes. For one of his haughty nature to be a dependant for so many years must have been a desperate humiliation. What a joy at last to kick his patron in the teeth! On the other hand, Germany, the enemy, was defeated. So Germany could be treated with condescension."

Blow winter winds blow. Thou are not as bitter as man's ingratitude. His rancour has certainly poisoned the European debate in Britain.

I think also of Raoul Nordling, the Swedish Consul who brokered the cease-fire and went through the German lines to fetch Allied help. Undoubtedly we have much to thank him for.

I turn away from the Hotel Meurice and walk north a few streets to where I am to install my Andrews Active Star. As usual on my visits to France, I've brought a couple of tea bags and some small cartons of U.H.T. milk. Not perfect by any means, but passable if you have a thirst on. And I have. Time for work.

In a sense, my journey doesn't end then, but a couple of days later, in the great cathedral of Beauvais. I've always loved churches, even if I am a bit of a fraud, being an agnostic. But there is something very calming in a church, and a particular symbolism in Catholic ones that I find very moving.
It is dark. I make my way forward to the lights of the altar. There, as so often (always perhaps) in Catholic churches, a number of candles are burning in a sand filled tray. They have been lit to the memory of the dead. I pay the few francs requested and light two more.

TO LIGHT THREE CANDLES

One is for Raoul Nordling. One is for Dietr von Choltitz. I bow my head, close my eyes, and thank them for their contribution to European, and my family's, life.

Then I realise that I have forgotten somebody, so I light a third. It is, of course, for the Parisienne who danced her wild jig with the trousers of the general officer of the Wehrmacht.

SELLING FRENCH DREAMS

The most important sale of all.
V.I.D.   Preparing for take off.

We had placed our house on the books of several of the notaires whom I know up and down the Cotentin peninsula. It is a beautiful house which, set in its large garden, is very photogenic. The photograph that appeared in the notaires' property magazine *Nota,* which is widely distributed in the area, did it justice.

We were prepared for a very long wait. Dick, for example, had been trying to sell his house for over a year. Even though he had dropped the price, and always made sure that it was at the top of the list of properties that he showed to prospective buyers, he had had little interest. He had learned, as have so many others, that buying a dream house in France is a rather easier process than selling it. In our case, however, fate was to be kind.

It was our own local notaire, Tatard et Mayeux, of Percy and Villedieu, who made the sale. The buyer was a lady from Avranches, just about to retire from the hospital there, and her partner. She had grown up in Percy, and wanted to come back to live near the town.

Unusually for the French, the couple wanted to live in the countryside. They both had children and grandchildren, so I think that the large garden attracted them. In fact, in that irrational way which people have with house purchase, I think that what sold the place was the swings.

Once started, the process went through very quickly. The lady visited first, alone, on a Thursday. On the Saturday she came again with her partner. On the Sunday, she visited with her daughter and her family. On the Monday she made an offer.

In the meantime we agonised over our decision.

Was our choice to return to England the right one, or should we move within France, to be nearer the French end of my work? The difficulty was to know where that would be. Currently I was working between London and Paris; in my next contract, I might be commuting between Leeds and Lyon.

Besides, contracting does not provide easy security of employment. Between one Anglo-French contract and the next, I might be 'resting' for several months. In that case, it was wise to be where I could pick up other bits of work to tide me over. That meant England. Added to that, with the kids well into school, Ann wanted to go back to work. England again.

We had a talk with the lady who was buying our house. Would she mind if we moved at the end of the school term, so that the kids could finish one term in France and start a new one back in England? (we were to move back to the same village in Buckinghamshire that we had moved from, two years before). She agreed. We accepted the price she offered. It was only slightly less than we had paid. Of course, we had to write off the money that we had spent on the place. And we automatically lost a packet because of the government tax and agency fees which we had paid. Another painful reminder that we should have rented. But it could have been a lot worse.

Apart from the usual horror-story of arranging a move; the packing, legal aspects, services, transport, cleaning, etc, etc, there was to be the added complication of animals. We were going to leave the cats with friends (they were getting on a bit and another move would probably have killed them). Which left Flavie. As I've said, Flavie is one of the pups of Zoe, the Jack Russell bitch which our neighbour, René, used to take to the fields on a little box on the back of his tractor.

René used to spoil Zoe rotten, feeding her with bits from the table, making a fuss. My own attitude towards Flavie is a little more restrained.

By and large, I quite like dogs. They're mostly very loving and trusting and dumb. Refreshing attributes after (most) cats and (many) humans. I'm less keen on dogs which make a fuss and chew up my post. Flavie, as a Jack Russell, comes into this category. However, with Ann it is very much 'love me, love my dog', so we were taking her to England, to six months' quarantine and, I suppose, to the home of her ancestors (unless Jack Russell is merely a mispronunciation of a French name, such as Jacques Rousseau).

We went through a flurry of farewells to our friends. We visited the primary school in Percy to thank the headmaster, Monsieur Brochard, for the excellent teaching that he and his staff had given Alice and David. The children, too, had their farewells to make, and collected a mass of addresses and telephone numbers. A stab of fear. What right did we have to drag our kids round like this?

Ann was to leave first with the children, to prepare our new home in England, while I was to stay behind a little longer to sign the completion contract. Then I would follow on with the dog. And so Ann, David and Alice left.

We spent a quiet couple of days, the poor old dog and I. For once that was quite a nice change. Of late, things had been a little hectic.

Finally, the day arrived. I went across the garden, pausing a moment at the pond. Then I walked through the gap in the hedge, over the road and round by René and Thérèse's milking parlour. There was the front door with the mimosa growing to one side. Lassie, their black mastiff, didn't bark as she used to. She was getting a little old now. I knocked on the ancient door. Thérèse answered. She was wiping her hands on a towel. We kissed the customary three times.

I went in to the kitchen for the last time. René was sitting on the bench at the kitchen table as I had seen him do a hundred times before. He had a bottle of calvados in front of him. Waiting for me.

"*Eh maintenant mes amis, il faut partir,*" I said sadly.

He nodded, his eyes for once grave. "We're sorry to see you go. It'll be quiet around here without you and Ann and the kids."

"Not for long. You'll be moving down into Percy yourselves in a couple of weeks."

"Ah yes, retirement. Everything changes."

Somehow we got along on that level. I thanked them for looking after us for the last couple of years. I turned down the calvados - for once - but accepted the coffee. Coffee gives me a headache, especially the black, heart-stopping thimble measures that the French drink. But I never refused it. It is a social contact first and foremost. Then it was time to go. I kissed Thérèse again, hugging her for a long moment.

René escorted me back to the road. I looked for one last time at the farmyard, with the nettles, the abandoned tractor, the old outhouse with its great *tonneaux* full of cider. My friend pressed a bottle of his best calvados on me as we parted. I shook hands with him. His eyes were full of tears.

"*Eh oui*," he said at last, "*c'est comme ca*." That's the way it is.

I turned away, I was in the same state as René. "We'll be back to see you."

And then I walked back to my house, put Flavie in the car, turned the key in the lock for the last time and drove away.

My next visit that day was to Pascal, the vet in Percy. Pascal and his wife, Nelly, were friends of ours. I had booked ahead, so Pascal was waiting for Flavie with the needle. "You know, *Alain*," he said thoughtfully, "I really don't see the need for this. There is no rabies in Normandy."

I turned on him angrily. "Maybe not, but there is in France. What if it got into our country?"

He shrugged. "And yet the rule does not apply to your horses which race in France. Why not simply vaccinate your pets six months before travelling? Then issue them with a certificate."

I did not know the answer to this, so I kept quiet.

The poor dog was more confused than ever (how could I ever have considered leaving her behind?), but soon she was asleep and in her basket. I shook hands with Pascal, put the basket in the car, and headed north to the ferry at Cherbourg.

It was a sunny day and pretty quiet on the roads. I arrived early at the ferry terminal, as I had been advised, and reported to the port office. I explained my business and two veterinary officers escorted me by a back route through the massive terminal to the ship, where we were loaded on before the other cars. Flavie was taken from me to be put in the quarantine cage, locked up somewhere in the depths below.

I went up on deck, and watched as the ferry began to fill up. Then we were off, sailing out through the breakwaters, past the forts. A couple appeared at my side, the man had a book in his hands and was talking to his wife:

"It's peaceful here now, but Cherbourg really went through it in the war. The Allies needed to capture the port to build up supplies after the landings. The Germans had remote controlled anti-aircraft guns sited on these breakwaters. They shot down eighty aircraft on the 25th of June 1944."

"It is my book you know," she replied.

The book was 'A Normandy Tapestry'.

"Is it good?" I asked the woman.

She answered me with a slight, very English, reserve: "Well, we've enjoyed it. I take it that you like France?"

"Yes, I like France."

She smiled, and the smile transformed her. "Then you might enjoy the book too. You can get it in the shop."

I smiled back. I was tempted to tell her that I had just ordered another three thousand copies of it. Of course I didn't, but I was very pleased.

I stood on the deck and looked out beyond the wake of the great ship towards the coast of France, slipping towards the horizon. I was taking stock. The country had been our home for the last two years. What had our family gained and lost by the experience?

The losses were easy to quantify. We were leaving behind a beautiful house and garden, such as we could never hope to afford in England.

And we had lost money. Going to France without a job had been an act of sheer financial folly. I had found the job, two in fact, but not the money. Still, I was earning money now by using the language, so that wasn't wholly a loss.

And anyway, money isn't everything. There had been gains. For me they were enormous. I had been behind the scenes of rural France and seen a lifestyle which I knew to be on the verge of disappearing. And I had seen a traditional way of farming that, sadly, it seemed would also soon become history; the clean, organic non-intensive methods that are given so much lip-service (but less financial support) today. I remembered a preview that I had read recently in *L'Express* magazine, for a television series about those farmers:

> "You watch them drinking their coffee at daybreak, from a bowl or a cup, eat in silence, welcoming a rare visit from a neighbour or a vet.
>
> It's easier to get into the High Court than onto a farm. You have to be very sensitive, the farming folk are a little fragile. Mistrustful, closed, some took three or six months before they would allow a camera in...."

I had had the privilege to get behind those closed doors. Far from being the monsters with two horns and a tail that I had been led to expect from the British press, I had liked those farmers, learned from them and found them worthy of respect. I hoped that I had shown it to them.

The children had benefited too. They could speak a second

language and had the tools to learn others, should they so wish.

And Ann? I've never asked her in so many words to draw up a profit and loss account. Whichever way the scales tipped for her, on the plus side she has her dog. Flavie is now, and was then, a V.I.D. A Very Important Dog.

Flavie and I were held-back until the rest of the ship had emptied (which explained why we had been put on first). The poor dog, groggy but coming out of the drug, was loaded into a cage in a great four-wheel drive quarantine wagon. With lights flashing and siren wailing, it led me through the streets of Southampton and northwards.

Finally we arrived at our destination, a quarantine kennels in Buckinghamshire. It was a series of old Nissen huts, surrounded by chain-link fencing, topped off with barbed wire. Each - locked - hut was divided into separate one-dog cells. Each cell door was locked from the outside. The only other way out of the cells was a run covered with wire. There were lights all around the perimeter. Appropriately enough, it had served as a Prisoner of War camp during the war.

Flavie served her six months, growing thinner all the time. Shortly after her release the quarantine rules were scrapped.

Lots of questions in the village: "Why did you come back?" Where to start to reply?

... ...

Time has passed since we came back from France. The kids have settled back into English school. Ann is working for the National Health Service. Life has treated me well since I passed my Diploma and started to use French in computer contracting. I have quite a few contracts under my belt, and I'm working between London and Paris again.

I am in London. It is an August morning and I am walking from Euston station to the English side of my contract, in Saint James' Square. It's great to be alive. I'm carrying an overnight bag, for I shall be in Paris tonight. I walk through the bus station, cross the Euston Road, pass through the alley by the Friends' Meeting House and head up past Virgina Woolf's house and towards the British Museum.

Today, I am excited, cock-a-hoop. There's no reason and every reason. My contract is coming to an end soon. Our bank balance is healthy once more; and I have decided to take a break and write a sequel to *A Normandy Tapestry*.

I pass the British Museum, turn, look in the window of the Egyptian shop (What worlds! what colour! what beauty!) and cross New Oxford Street. It is 8.20 A.M. and the streets are quiet. I smile. It's going to be a superb day.

I've learned a lot about books and publishing in the last couple of years I have reprinted *A Normandy Tapestry* twice and it looks as if I will need to reprint it again. Of all the things I had to get right for that book, I think the one I boobed on was the title. Clever me. I've met more than one person who has thought that it was a book about needlework. While there may be confused ladies who bought it for that reason, and who are wondering when the detailed instructions start, I'm sure there are many more who have left it on the shelf for the same reason. The title of my new book? Something snappier for sure. I'm toying with 'Selling Dreams' - Dick's term for the process of selling French property. We'll see.

I walk briefly along Drury Lane - where the Great Plague started - and take a dog-leg to the Charing Cross Road. In the distance is St Martin's in the Fields. What a wonderful name for a church; even if it is in Trafalgar Square. London is waking up; but not with a bad temper. London rarely has a bad temper. I love that.

So, take some time off, write that book. It's an exciting (and daunting) prospect. I walk past the sleeping Chinese restaurants and under the plane trees in Leicester Square. Round the back of the National Gallery and past the concrete car park where once the Royal tennis court stood. Over Haymarket. A red double-decker stops for me at the crossing.

When the book is done, then I've promised myself a cycling holiday with a pal of mine. By then, I will be in need of exercise. We will travel as foot passengers on the ferry, then cycle from Cherboug to Saint Malo. It'll be a bit of an adventure. I've never cycled anything like as far before.

Accommodation will not be a problem. There are plenty of *Chambres d'Hote's* (B & B's) and small country hotels on our route. They don't cost a lot; and some of them are real corkers. There are chateaux - some pristine, some a little run-down (which I prefer). There are farm houses lost in the *bocage* with great long tables, where you all eat together, the booze flows like water, and the food is second-to-none. There are small-town hotels where you ring the bell and wander corridors for ages before tracking Madame or Monsieur the proprietor down. There are ancient manors where the clock seems to have stopped a century or two back.

We'll sample one or two of these delights, I'm sure; but mostly it looks as if we'll be staying with friends down the peninsula. That will mean there'll be some business along with the bicycling; but I've told Roger - who I'm going with - my planned itinerary and he hasn't been put off.

I've found that I'm not the only small publisher about France.

I know of six others now. We'll visit one of them who lives near Cherbourg. We have lots to talk about; lots of plans. Then we'll visit our friends Brigitte and her husband Jerome at St Lo, then René and Thérèse in Percy. I'm going to see if I can get René to arrange a trip out on a trawler. To watch the fishing and hopefully see some dolphins.

If the book's ready by then, I shall pop into the primary school at Percy and give a copy of it to the headmaster.

The next day, we'll go for lunch with Peter Edwards. I intend to sound him out. Many people have asked me for advice over the years about living and working in France: would Peter be interested in starting the course up again?

We shall visit my notaire friend too. I want to have a look through his property books. I've half a mind to 'Do a *Marchand de Biens*'. He's promised to take me to one of those 'candle' auctions; where all the bidding must be completed between the time a short candle is lit and it burns out. I'll offer to build him a web site (Prefecture permitting). He has some interesting properties. If he wants an agent in England, I will try a couple of them on my own site. I may end up selling French houses again. Selling houses, not dreams.

After my experiences to date with selling French property, that might seem surprising. A bit as if a dim-witted tourist who has taken a weekend break at the Assassins' castle and miraculously escaped with his life were to book in for a further night. It must be the 'biggin' in me.

Then we'll stay a night or two with David and Glynis, English friends with a small-holding who have weathered many a storm and who have a host of tales to tell. Comfortable company. After that, it's into Brittany. I intend to visit a couple of bookshops on the way. I must improve the French distribution of my books (or it may be that there will be more than just my books, depending on how discussions with the other small publishers pan out).

It promises to be a rather interesting trip. I'll let you know how I get on.

I've reached Saint James' Square now. I cut the corner, walking past the flowers where the poor policewoman was shot from the (ex) embassy window, and through the great doors of the office. Not bad. Two miles, thirty five minutes. I hear Alice's clear, piping voice from the past, and smile a little sadly:

"*Cinq kilomètres à pied,*
ca roul-a, ca roul-a..."

"Passports please."

The morning has passed and I am at Heathrow Airport. My work in Paris is on the south side of the city, making driving impractical. I'm about to catch the flight for Orly. I am in the standard English uniform, dark suit and tie. If I'd been going straight from home, I would have been more casual, like the French. I fish my passport out from my inside pocket, hand it over and am given a boarding card.

"Thank you sir. ....sir, I think you've dropped something." I look down. There, on the ground, are a dozen or so little square multi-coloured pieces of card, sealed by an elastic band. My English-French learning scheme. I pick them up and hurry through the boarding gate and towards the plane.

"Paper sir? Telegraph, Mail?"

I select a newspaper and sit down. I'll look at it in a minute. I've a job to do first. I take the cards out of their elastic band. Ann gave them to me, with the strict instructions to do them on the plane. I don't know what she's up to; but where women are concerned, experience had taught me that it's generally wisest to do what I'm told. They're a very random mixture, due to the fact that for cat-related reasons my entire stock of Anglo-French cards fell from the spare bedroom window last night and scattered up the road, doubtless confirming many neighbourly suspicions as I used various strategies to retrieve them. Some are yonks old; some recent. Some are the kids', some mine.

"Fasten your seat belts Ladies and Gentlemen."

Then the plane is rolling down the concrete runway. Ker-clump, ker-clump, ker-clump, ker-clump. Faster and faster.

'I like to play on the computer and listen to music.' David's.

A couple of very basic cards, 'walk' and 'the food'. Flavie's perhaps.

'I am a vegetarian, but I eat fish.' Alice's.

An increase of engine power. A funny feeling in the pit of my stomach. Now a few cards which are definitely my own, a funny mixture of grammatical oddities, proverbs and bits I've culled from books:

Des serpents! Je les ai vus au bord de la route. 'I've seen some snakes by the side of the road': An obscure one: what could I have been reading to provide that gem?

Reculer pour mieux avancer. Ah! This is even more difficult. I've translated it as 'strategic retreat', but that's not quite right; it's a little too military. In trying to translate it perfectly, I've hunted around a bit, and it seems to be from Lao Tzu, a Taoist philosopher. Following that thread was valuable in its own right; but still didn't lead me to an exact translation. Anyway, the idea is that sometimes you have to go back first if you want to go forward. I can verify that well enough.

There's only one card left now. I pick it up.

Of course my dreams - my new book and the other vague thoughts and half-formed plans that I have - may come to nothing. I can but try. Effort and planning, however, though you can't get far without them, are no guarantee of success in this world. You've got to do a good job, of course: but you need a bit of luck too. But coming across this card at this time - whether my wife planted it there or not - seems like a good omen.

At the end of the cards, Ann has folded in a scrap of paper. So this is what she was up to! It's a shopping list, such as I'm always given on these trips. In domestic circumstances, I am a wooden head. It's completely pointless to tell me what is needed. It has to be spelled out. So here it is. What to buy on my trip. Benco (a chocolate drink) for David. I'll need to find a small supermarket for that. Hollywood chewing gum ('as many flavours as you can') for Alice. Yes, I can get that from the *boulangerie*. Goats's cheese for Ann. Hm. I will have to buy that immediately before catching the plane back, and hope that it doesn't melt on the way.

On the bottom of the list there are little private messages from my wife and children. They would mean nothing to anybody else, but they make me smile. In fact they make me laugh out loud. To hell with the doubts and fears. It is one of those rare moments when I realise just how well-off I actually am.

The businessman in the next seat looks at me a little oddly. But that doesn't shut me up. I just laugh louder as the message sinks in. I wish my wife was with me now, so that I could tell her that I think that whatever battles lie ahead, we've already won the main one. My neighbour buries his head in his newspaper.

The plane leaves the ground.

SELLING FRENCH DREAMS

Re-ordering

If you have enjoyed this book and think that a friend might also enjoy it, don't lend it to them! What nicer, more personal and reasonably-priced gift than a signed copy of their own? Copies of *A Normandy Tapestry* are also available. There are two ways that you can get signed copies:

1. You can order by sending a cheque to:
> Kirkdale Books,
> 16 Weston Road, Great Horwood,
> MK17 0QQ, Buckinghamshire.

Price: *Selling French Dreams*: £9
A Normandy Tapestry: £8. Both together £15
Add £1 if to go outside the U.K, otherwise postage free.
The book/s can be mailed to your address, or direct to the recipient along with a card saying who it is from.

Please state:
> Which book you want.
> The address it is to be posted to.
> The message to go on the attached card (if appropriate).
> Make your cheque payable to Kirkdale Books

2. Signed copies are also available at the book's website:
www.normandy-tapestry.com
The site also has links to other French-related sites.

Or you can order copies from most bookshops.

Appendix.

The thirteen reefs.

Buying property
- Buying an isolated house
- Underestimating renovation costs: Mike's rules:
  Get quotes.
  Make sure that the specification of work is complete. If the customer isn't clear about what he (or she) wants doing, the builder won't be either.
  If uncertain, get a survey done.
  Always add a contingency to costings.
  Make sure that builders are aware of French standards. If the work isn't done to those standards (particularly electrical), fire insurance will be invalidated.
  Find out if planning permission is needed. If so, get it.

- Buying with the wrong legal entity (example: using an SCI to buy if intending to pursue a commercial activity). See the letter by Pat Willis, below.
- Not putting the correct suspensive clauses in the sales agreement (example: not saying you intend to use the property for business)

Moving and everyday life
- Getting a *Carte de Sejour* (residency permit). You need to prove that you will not be a drain on French systems before you can legally live there.
- Health insurance

For those with children
- Childrens' education

For those doing business

- Running out of money
(getting timing, costs or income projections wrong)
- Working illegally
Whether this is because you have been incompetently advised, or whether you have not done the necessary homework, it is you who will suffer the consequences.
- Not having a market for the product
- Not marketing the business successfully

Social (everybody)

- Learning the language
- Making friends

Recommendations for those considering moving to France. (based on a survey of 106 British people already living there)

Recommendation	%	posn.
Rent before you buy	99	1
Learn French. Start before you move	95	2
Integrate and live French	85	3
Make friends	80	4
Be financially solvent	60	5
Be wary of people	45	6
Plan carefully, don't just daydream	40	7
Don't be isolated physically	40	7
Try and receive British T.V.	30	9
Be prepared for culture shock	25	10
Don't bring children over the age of 7	20	11
Have a fall-back position	15	12

A Nightmare in Normandy - by Pat Wallis

A year in Provence? Child's play! Peter Mayle should try
eighteen months in Normandy. We have and survived to tell
the tale, albeit verging on insanity.

We are an ill-assorted conglomerate of Northern Brits - two
teachers, a marine engineer and a gofor who have become
the increasingly humble proprietors of a derelict farmhouse, a
number of dubious outbuildings and a hectare of weeds and
thistles in Fresue la Mère outside Falaise.

You may well ask why. We do, regularly. All we know is that
we sent our partners to France to seek out a small house to
renovate in the region of the Loire and 80,000 francs. They
returned with a heap of rubble in Normandy in the region of
800,000 francs. When we came to see it, it was raining so hard
our brains went rusty and we agreed to the purchase.

There was a spark of method in our madness. The main
farmhouse was to provide accommodation after early
retirement, for both couples, which would be subsidised by the
letting of the renovated outbuildings to English holiday makers.
This plan was to be realised over 5-10 years with the help of
a friendly French bank manager and the sale of a less decrepit
weavers' shed in Yorkshire.

Our real problems began when we tried to 'get legal'.

Following legal advice, we purchased the property in May
1991 by means of an S.C.I. (*Societe Civile Immobilier* - often
used in purchasing to avoid problems with inheritance laws).
A year ago, in the wake of several horrendous estimates for
the first phase of development, I innocently trundled along to
a local accountant to enquire into the possiblity of reclaiming
TVA on the building.

After the statutory sharp intake of breath, he made a few
rapid and incomprehensible telephone calls at the end of
which I was taken to Caen for a meeting with various members

of a *Cabinet Fiduciare*. The fact that the meeting consisted of five men in business suits and myself, a mere woman in her painting clothes - left me at a serious disadvantage. The outcome of the two hour meeting (with a hefty bill) was that an S.C.I. was not permitted to engage in commercial activity.

They were not yet agreed where we should go from here, despite reading each other long passages from large legal tomes and arguing about them. They would, however, re-assess the matter and honour us with the gift of their expert advice at some future date (subject to invoice).

Thus we had instituted an SCI, bought a property, rendered the main house almost fit for human habitation, rendered the outbuildings unfit for rat habitation, settled a date in October when the previous incumbent would definitely remove his cows from the milking parlour and unwittingly entered a morass of legal and fiscal complications. We went back to Yorkshire to plan and dream.

Glossary.

SCI - a method of avoiding the complications of French inheritance laws, thereby embroiling oneself in the complications of French business law.

TVA - VAT and then some.

Cabinet Fiduciare - a collection of financially minded gentlemen who consider that small business should contribute as little as possible to the taxman and as much as possible to themselves.

Helpful hints so far

Discover the legal and financial implications of any proposed plan before buying the property. Find out beforehand what professional help will be required and approximate cost.

Keep away from French accountants whenever possible.

(I have not been able to trace Pat Wallis and I hope she doesn't mind me quoting her letter. Should she wish to get in touch with me, I will gladly send her a couple of books to acknowledge an excellently written and very useful letter).

Staying in Touch.

For those intending moving to France ...
The chapter 'The Dangerous Crossing' and the appendix are intended to give a full map of all the 'reefs' that can ruin your move to France; but it is neither a two day course, nor a book on the subject.

I have written mainly about education, fitting in socially and learning the language. I have barely touched on those areas which are generally covered by standard books on the subject. For example, I have mentioned health, but not discussed this very jagged 'reef' at all. In time, I hope to put more on these subjects on my website (see below). In the meantime, I can recommend:

Living and working in France. Survival Books
David Hampshire ISBN 1-901130-55-X

Buying a Home in France. Survival books. David Hampshire ISBN 1-901130-90-8

Your comments.
I like to get feedback on my books, so feel free to write or email. If what you say is of general interest, I may add it to my web site (so please say if you don't want to be quoted).

My address:
    Alan Biggins, Kirkdale Books,
    16 Weston Road, Great Horwood,
    Bucks, MK17 0QQ
email me: mail@normandy-tapestry.com
website: www.normandy-tapestry.com